Across

MIRAGE OF LIFE

VOLUME II

SATHEESAN RANGORATH

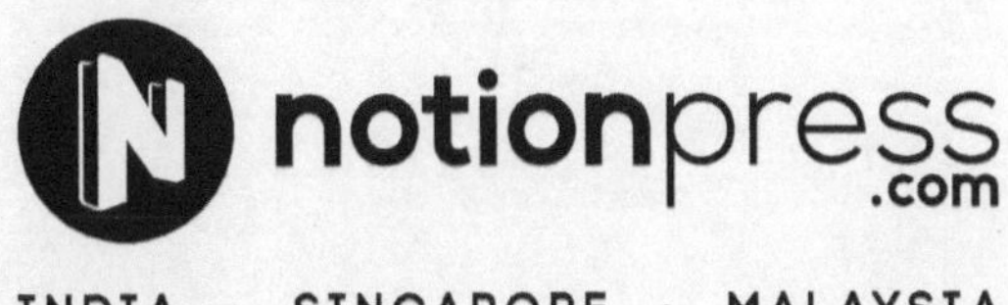

INDIA • SINGAPORE • MALAYSIA

Copyright © Satheesan Rangorath 2023
All Rights Reserved.

ISBN 979-8-89026-786-3

This book has been published with all efforts taken to make the material error-free after the consent of the author. However, the author and the publisher do not assume and hereby disclaim any liability to any party for any loss, damage, or disruption caused by errors or omissions, whether such errors or omissions result from negligence, accident, or any other cause.

While every effort has been made to avoid any mistake or omission, this publication is being sold on the condition and understanding that neither the author nor the publishers or printers would be liable in any manner to any person by reason of any mistake or omission in this publication or for any action taken or omitted to be taken or advice rendered or accepted on the basis of this work. For any defect in printing or binding the publishers will be liable only to replace the defective copy by another copy of this work then available.

Dedication

I dedicate this collection ACROSS MIRAGE OF LIFE in loving memory of my departed wife Saroja Satheesh (Saru). She had helped me come through many hard times while she was succumbing to fate. May this Taj Mahal of words be a mausoleum created by an unknown person to an unknown person.

Contents

EMERALD

Foreword

My friend Satheesan Rangorath is an earnest writer of poetry in both English and Malayalam. That he has already published a mega volume of 3000 odd poems couple of years back is a testimony of his deep routed interest in expressing his opinions, reactions and intuitive experiences in verse. I am reminded of the famous words of William Blake, *"To see a world in a grain of sand and heaven in a wildflower; Hold infinity in the palm of your hand and eternity in an hour."*

He has been part of few international poetry forums where he had been sharing his poems in English, most of them have brought him ecstatic appreciation and most of them have been grouped under top billings of gold, silver, emerald etc. An essential precondition for being able to appreciate the expression of a poet, is to have an open mind of a virtually blank sheet of white paper. Spontaneous reaction and appreciation arises from this point of view, the international forum of poems must have found the import of the original eastern thoughts and expression of Satheesan to their liking.

Satheesan was in deep love with his beloved wife for nearly 5 decades, emphasises the outlook of a person who sees and values of life in their true shades. It then follows that he has penned many of his poems in the light of their mutual love and bonding. The sad demise of his wife Saroja two years back has left him in a pall of gloom although the spiritual strength that he derives from his guru Matha AmrithanathaMayi (Amma) has been sustaining him in the right spirit.

It may not be possible to take a tour of the 100s of poems that he has penned to review critically, though most of them deserve a look up. One striking feature is however is his infinite attachment to his departed wife that keeps surfacing from his memories and over runs the flow of other inspiring subjects. A rare outpour that strikes as over whelming is when he says, "Each letter was carved from the depth of my thoughts, erected a mansion adorned with selected artefacts Don't know when you will find it, may be trade wings carry it up to you ...." and the flow of his thoughts continues with equal depth". The depth of his pain while featuring the war-torn areas of Ukraine, the focus is on the Ambarnaya river which he paints as strips in red what with the massive oil pollution, "She is just a young girl turned into puberty–they deflowered her near the Russian city of Norilsk in Siberia". The reflection of his subtle meditative observation of his Guru Matha Amritananta Mayi, he expresses his experience thus, "once she said; in the end, there is nothing but a bit smile, end of knowledge and beginning of wisdom". The smile is beatific, decidedly. His imagination runs wild and captures a thought of a "Thanksgiving theme" where he pens thus; "he had oceaning dreams, life swam in the water. Birds land over the sea, fishes become foods for birds. Giant monster land over the earth".

A humorous fling on business channels where 'breaking news' of these channels has become the order of the day; he brands them as armchair journalism thinning out into the yellow media. He paints it little more vividly when he says "Often the judges that deliver judgments kill and create celebrities, the thief becomes a saint and the saint becomes a thief." Under the caption 'great barrier reef' his paint brush takes a meaningful swipe across the canvas when he says, "A heritage hiding in the Coral Sea meditating in the severity, silent chanting..... Dreaming in the paradise lost" In a subtler take on "aromatic autumn", he says "dreams hibernate, opening of fresh pink faces sprouts......how do I catch the picture of this exotic painting....." Reflecting his thoughts under the caption 'Android dream' the thoughts takes an imaginative run at a speed that mind only can generate, 'Suddenly my android lands on a bumpy ramp......................... Gliding like a fashion model placing a footprint on the martian land spraying and playing holi colours. About the ownership of this earth, he sketches with his pen painfully reflecting on the wars and consequential effect of slavery and wide spread damage to the peace lovers and closes with a helpless tail-peace with prophetic words, "One day you will have a shock, a cultural shock............in the annals of history you live as arsonists and extortionists, war mongers of modernity".

Satheesan is a serious thinker and reacts inwardly to situations in life although being a non-controversial person that he is, his impressions often find expression in words in his poems. The topics that bear out of this attribute cover a wide range of common day situations as political, social personal, interpersonal, cultural and spiritual. "I do not know what I am looking for with along tickling tongue. May be an entry to your soul I, have my tongue print on you as an id card". Or for that matter he writes in one instance, "when I write a poem it's a dream come true: from the silence of the mind, from the deep slumber of thoughts I discover a word, an image, or a soul full feeling of glitter." This should reveal the pen picture of a poet who finds expression of his thoughts and impressions of the world through poems, an average of more than one per day. He is on the eve of releasing his latest volume of poems of few thousands. I wish him all the best and may he continue to inspire and impress the world of poetry lovers for a long time to come.

Brig Narayan Menon (Retd)

Author's Note

May I present this anthology of my poems with humility before the reading intelligentsia Many of these poems are participants in various competitions conducted by a US-based poetry site named Allpoetry. com. There are five categorised sections according to the medals they won from the competition as Gold, Silver, Bronze and Emerald. A few are under general categories which were applauded by the host. However, I am leaving it to the reader (if any!) to judge.

We were rowing our boat together in troubled waters. The river flooded several times rocking our raft severely yet, we managed the rudder steady and kept the mast adjusted to the flow of wind. The river was streaming at the high spate.

Somewhere beyond the time we travelled to the time and dived through many lives, discarded our clothes many times. Carried carryovers of Karma from previous births, the burden was heavy, the sack was full.

At a different point in time, we were born. Destiny united us in human life as husband and wife. We were bound together with wedlock. Since then, we had our happy moments, good times, and bad times. It was also our fate that had forbidden us from having more attachments as our children. Me and Saru (Saroja) and accepted the reality we became a child to each other and looked after well. Time took out us to different scenes and scenarios. We could adjust mutually to the hard facts of life. However, no complaints we respected each other, and I was not an overbearing husband. She was gentle and cute and approved of all my decisions. All her suggestions were honoured in our day-to-day life.

I was having a good bank job in the United Arab Emirates. Greed did not attack us. My job was enough for both of us and our future family.

We decided to be peaceful at home having only one earning member. I met all her desires and commitments without any grumbling. The purse was common. She hardly had any requirements. Even jewellery and comforts were all reasonable and judged. She had an aversion for show and display, which she might have imbibed from my character. We were happy and had our fights too.

Life took us to different modes. Like any newly married we desired to have our kids. However, we realised the reality after 12 years of treatment often visits to infertility clinics. Frustration and pressure gave us a down spirit after the abortion of the first pregnancy. Again continuing the treatment was depressing and traumatic for her. We decided not to and decided to return home. I was in my 50s and Saroja was 40. We settled in Palakkad without any regrets. Shortly after she was ill with a compressed disc problem. Bedridden for 3 months. from there onwards, our struggle with diseases started ending up with a Renal problem. The treatment continued for 18 years. In the meantime, I had to undergo bypass surgery and a carsova of bladder problems.

Despite all, we had our good times too. Proudly I can say I took her to many countries as a tourist. We visited Abu Dhabi, Dubai, my former place of employment. Then to Singapore and Malaysia. The land of wonders placed our footprints at Change international airport. Singapore. Visiting Marina Singapore giant wheel gave us a lasting impression of the city. Touching the feet of Lord Muruga we visited the Batu cave in Malaysia and then to Genting heights where we put our feet in the largest hotel in the world First World Hotel. Birds park, orchid garden. We returned to India with a long-lasting impression and a craving for more travel.

Next year we took a vacation to Europe, starting from London, A historic city on the banks of the Thames river, the Land of merchants and political feuds. A country of great writers, scholars, and world-famous universities. A city associated with Indian leaders like Gandhi and Nehru. Unforgettable London eye on the banks of river Thames. Smooth streaming river filled with Cruise ships and boats. Several overhead bridges connecting both banks are littered with historical buildings. we had a memorable cruise on the river. We witnessed Big ben, parliament house, and Westminster Abbey. Buckingham palace. Overnight cruise to the Netherlands world's Tulip garden, Rotterdam, Amsterdam, and Hague. Our bus was waiting to take us to the selected European countries. Belgium chocolate street, artificial diamonds, Austria zavrouski crystals showroom. In Austria, we stayed in a 400-year-old wooden hotel. We're living through history. Liechtenstein, a small country between Austria and Switzerland memory ligers, we shopped for a small memento, a collapsible cup, which Saroja kept in her bag handy. Through the tunnels of Alphs, we reached France. The ancient beautiful city of Paris, the city of lights, the Eifel tower, intricate architecture flawless engineering. My wife bought some scarves of silk from the hawkers near the tower as a souvenir for our Paris visit. Placed a rose on the under path where Princess Diana had her last trip. Most photographed Élysée Palace, palace and garden. the seine river cruise was another milestone in memory lane. Again our bus took us to Italy. The first city we visited was Florence. The city of painters and artisans. Great. Leonardo Davinci and Michelangelo, of Italy We paid our silent respects to these renowned masters. Venice is a wonderful piece of heaven on earth." Ponte delle Guglie, Ponte dei Tre Archi is unique among the bridges of Venice for its design; there used to be a few other three-arched bridges in the city, but this is the only one that has survived to this day. 11. Ponte dei Bareteri" Most Famous Bridges in Venice Bridge of Sighs. This infamous footbridge connects the Doge's Palace with the Prigioni (prisons). Though many visitors... Rialto Bridge. Glass blower's gallery took us by surprise. Very exquisite display of vases and other artefacts Salutations to those artisans. The Vatican is another small city-state. RevH.H Pope Francis was on rounds in his pope mobile. We visited the Sistine chapel.

Thrilled to see the ceiling paintings of Davinci

In 2018 we took another tour of the Peoples Republic Of China, Hong Kong and Macau. We visited the forbidden city of Royalty, the Temple of Heaven, and the Doomed silence of Tianmin square. Sounds of the Bootfall of soldiers, the helpless cry of students who fought for freedom daringly. There Saroja had a lasting memory. She endured and walked the entire parade ground about two KM or more barefooted. Her slipper strap had broken there were no shops in that area she took it sportingly and walked through. Even she made a friendship with a janitor woman and secured herself an old sandal for the rest of the city round tour. She kept it as a souvenir after coming back. The memories of the great wall of china and the pride we could reach there, from the words of high school history books. The fast-growing shanghai city is a very picturesque modern city, we visited the shanghai tower and had a bird's eye view of the city. The Everlasting experience of bullet train rides The 1931km high-speed railway links Shanghai and Hong Kong. There is only one high-speed train G99 from Shanghai Hongqiao Railway Station to Hong Kong West Kowloon Railway Station at 02:10 PM every day. The duration is 8 hours and 18 minutes.

In Hong Kong, the remarkable visit was to Victoria Peak The peak tram is a funicular railway in Hong Kong, which carries both tourists and residents to the upper levels of Hong Kong Island. Running from Garden Road Admiralty to Victoria Peak via the Mid-Levels, it provides the most direct route and offers good views over the harbour and skyscrapers of Hong Kong. Hydrofoil ferry takes you to Macau in 45 mins. The land of casinos and 7-star hotels

All these travel notes I am writing to say that it was a great achievement for me and Saroja. despite our illness, I had bypass surgery and Saroja's deteriorating kidney disease was a challenge for both of us. In the previous paragraph, I forgot to add Saroja could travel in a cable car to Mount Titlis in Switzerland where the temperature was -20 celsius at that time. I made an Ice idol of Lord Ganesh. On the Ice hill.

Next year we took out vacation to Australia.. while floating in a hot air balloon In Cairnes We were scaling a negative mind to positivity. We got our first hot air ballooning certificate from Australia.

While rowing through the dark caves of glow worms we achieved another remarkable experience of fantasy. A speed boat ride was another adventure that I took to Saroja in New Zealand. The thrill was that I did not tell her that we were going on an adventure cruise. She was surprised that she had gone through the ride courageously.

There are many experiences to write about, but this is just a writeup of words built on the tomb of my wife, a " Taj Mahal of Jade". I erect this Sculpture of words in the unvisited celestial garden in my heart and soul.

I don't know I lost. still, my chest heaves her breathe last sound of pumping feeble with her moan. A short whisper strained whistling nostrils, parting grief eyes, wide a silent trickle of pain unable to hear her gestures to console. My legs faltered fear consumed poring cold sweat shivering shaking hands and legs. On my lap, she rested her head her last.....grip

I was helpless and did not have the penance to go behind Yamadharma Raja. I am not Nachiketa to follow Yama to Dharma Puri in order to get Saroja out. No one heard my cry at the odd hour of that black dawn. complete silence, my teardrops frozen Still, Now I am crying silently on my lonely nights and stillness of dawn every day calling the names of the lord.

These words in the poetry collection are my respectful homage to my wife Saroja. Probably the writings of an insignificant Pen to an unknown person. After all who will remember my wife after my departure? There is no hope of anyone doing any annual Balikarma for us. This is an epithet on the tomb of two unknown individuals who visited this earth for a short time and returned to infinity.

In the loneliness we used to watch the sunrise and diving sun together. She left yesterday leaving me alone and aloof. When this long wait will end?

Left me alone saw it all closing of a dream curtain down, we were talking about plans for dialysis, transplant, and donors, for my further... suddenly my breath stopped eyes were half closed am I in a psychedelic vision panicky sounds dressed to the hospital siren of an ambulance hopeful blue beacon light She was holding my hands pressing the chest to straighten, collapsed hands, dangling neck, sweat on forehead wiped by a hairy hand, breath stopped one inhalation and the last exhalation. Moon just disappeared leaving black clouds an owl busily turned his head and fluttered away into the darkness. Helpless shouts, cries, helpless sighs my dear I gave her resuscitation sprinkled with cold water yet, she had reached another world of brilliance left me alone.

A Passionate hug A passionate hug, I hear your heart, Your heartbeat, the chirp of your soul. Lovebird sings. I hear mine too. Through soft music, song of souls. Lovebirds sing. Together we hear the Symphony of millions, the music of souls. Echo of spirits, Deep in and out, vibrate in rhythm, love boundless. In the ocean of love, One with the cosmos, We merge in every atom, one soul; one song. I embrace, merging in oneness. I breathe in Breathe out. Turning into a dream, I fly high, and as I float, my wings cover the entire universe. We disappear In subtle softness. When you call I reverberate, from silence world around reply to my wish! End my monologue

I PLACE MY FLOWERS OF WORDS AT THE FEET OF MY BELOVED SAROJA, THE LOTUS

PRANAMAM

Aum Amriteswaryei namaha
Pranam to my beloved Guru H.H. Mata Amritanandamayi Devi, She is
my inspiration and Muse Saraswathi Devi
Aum Namashivaya.
Satheesan Rangorath

About the Author

Born to parents M.Sreedharan Nair, and Sarada Amma, Satheesan Rangorath completed his early education in the schools of his village, Elappulli in Palakkad District of Kerala, India. He graduated in Commerce from the Government Victoria College Palakkad. About this time he migrated to Bombay in search of a job, a feature common to many youngsters in those days. This is a looking back to the Path he trekked from 19/Nov/1948. As a simple observer of life, he has said many interesting things in simple vocabulary. His poems are not complicated and readable to any layman, who has basic knowledge of English. Quiet and generally reserved from his early days, he had found the power of poetry as a profoundly satisfying form of expression in a world that cannot stop talking. His intuitive response to the varieties of life situations interwoven with the mysteries of mother nature has aided the creative flow from within, helping himself to ink the lines in his leisure hours as a routine from his youth.

He graduated in law in 1978 before he moved to the United Arab Emirates where he served as a bank officer for 27 years. Supporting him in all walks of life has been his beloved wife, Saroja, a soft-spoken and able homemaker. In the year 2021 December 19, she left her heavenly abode. And this collection of his poem" ACROSS MAIRAGE OF LIFE IS" HIS HOMAGE AND DEDICATION IN MEMORY OF HIS BELOVED WIFE. Satheesan Rangorath has published his poems in many poetry forums and has received several accolades. " MEMORY SPROUTS" VOL I, II AND III his SECOND Publication. found entry into record books, India Book Of Records and Asia book of Records in the year. SNAPSHOTS OF A FIREFLY was his first published work of poems.

It is a huge collection of poems painted on a vast canvas. His bristly strokes are." Across mirage of life" is his third publication a poetry Mausoleum in memory of his wife Saroja Satheesh become a signature of his soulful vision across mirage of life.

Bronze

Secret Recipe

Once my grandma cooked a soup.
nobody knew the recipe
but it was a delicious delicacy
a mixture of hot, sweet, salty n' sour
we, the children, sipped it full
licked even sediments
by waggling tongue in the bowl.
ingredients were kept a secret
we thought it was her love
that tasted good.
no, it was her sour and salty
short temper in the form of
well wish that made it tasty
she gave us the potion with a
a mixture of her warmth.

at last one day, she revealed
her secret.
it was nothing but thick rice water
after cooking the rice in the water
she removed the cooked rice with a sieve,
kept the thick liquid for soup
she mixed vegetables, curd,
then enough salt and pepper,
seasoned with coconut oil and sugar.
that was her special soup
her soulful creation
adding her compassion and love.

Droplets

Honey, honey
my thoughts
is the honey
that was hidden
inside
pods of mind.
I create images
dipping in honeydew
of my imagination.
like a bee
I suck
and fill the syringe.
my simile
and metaphors
are injected
with celestial nectar,
to decorate your
lips with
droplets of love.

Fantasy

girlies three
in ravishingly
laced wears.
me
untied a knot
of fantasy.
you came out
in birthday suits
blowing
candles.

Good Morning

He took a slow dive
disintegrated his entity
ocean consumed him
covering his effulgence

the cocoon of silk
spun a dark thread around him
he was cocooned
in the labyrinth of time

thick saliva of darkness
fell on earth
far in the cloudy night sky
fangs of fear vomit
poisonous fumes

the world just woke up
from a nightmare
rooster crowing louder
slowly sun uncovers
the blanketed face
a flint of rays beams out

By rubbing his eyes
he got up to another day
good morning

Wisdom Begins

The one who has seen
never talks
the one who talks never
seen
where knowledge ends
wisdom begins
he spreads a fragrant
vibration
honeybees arrive
in search of honey
love percolates
from divinity
See you next summer
abrupt
Uncomfortable
silence
seeps everywhere.
not a single life-form around.
a blue shine glaze
all through the ice-capped valley.
slowly a breeze is forming.
suddenly face turns dark
white puffy snowy clouds
run over hoofing like
wild horses on the run
Bison on rampage

snowflakes afloat
visibility zero.
a long shrill whistle blow
from all directions.
unsecured roof tiles fly away
G I sheets float like missiles.
a hail shower.
roof top bombarded
fearful hum and howl
of wild elephants.
A Yeti walks tall
shaking the
planet.
I cover myself
in my sleeping bag
cuddled
as a polar bear
see you next summer.

5 / 7 / 5 / 7 / 7
Tanka [Howl of a Monster]

howl of a monster
quick landslide under the feet
mind, body, cascade
you float on the plunge basin
hoping for a string of hope

Snapshots

I do not wish to be known as a cliche poet
trekking the beaten path of forerunners
all alone in the crowd I watch and observe
my silence captures everything eloquently

sometimes I feel and curse my scanty words
my lexicon is limited to the extent of the moment
somehow I find my glossary float to the occasion
I select only the vocabulary that I am familiar

I am a firefly searching with a tiny bit of light
whatever I find clicked into my heart straight
I put those pictures into use as and when needed
I just take a simple snapshot of the subject

maybe those pictures were of aeons older
many are shot unaware of the requirements
and when I am creating with an inspiration
those images flash wildly in my mind and thoughts

with ease, they fall on my paper and pen
often I found my muse playing with me
she fulfilled my shortfalls with an elegant smile
holding her hands I reach for the star-studded sky

she used to carry me on her wings of imagery
I do not do anything, she creates a sculpture
before I get down to the world of reality
she winks at me while she departs for my dream

Nine Facial Expressions

From the abyss of the heart
from the colours of her thoughts
she mixed paints in the palette
of her mind
pastel hues depicted her moods
she paraded
her vision of life
in the sketches she made
and used every shade
as a meaning
hidden
behind the usage of paints
watercolours
flowed taking shapes
in great images
life was colour-coded
in her canvas
nine*
basic facial expressions
emerged from her brush
is on display
from the buildings
on the easel

Navarasas*

For Her Grace

I am in a trance, levitating above the world
when I am, I do not see anything
I murmur like possessed
senses conceive it remains in the pregnancy.
every sound is a song for me
I foresee things in subtle forms
a state of the surge, I have to write what I saw
what I heard, what I feel, I seclude
in my workshop scribbling my poem.
my muse watches me, tickling my senses
I am in love with the subject
I sculpt my images, my idols are adorned
I listen to her, I hear her silent chat.
finally, I come out, carry her in my soul
adore my divine lady, bow my head
placing my pen before her for her grace.

A Pathfinder

Dense darkness is consuming the world.
we live in fear of being consumed
from the secluded loneliness, you see,
several horrifying masks are worn over time.
fear vibes shake your limbs numb.
perspiration pours down your forehead.
a danger hiding beneath each footfall.
suddenly a firefly lit your pathway, a pathfinder

An Imaginative Retreat

I was on a beaten path
strewn with footprints
was searching something
what am I looking for?

I reached a dead end
that was my turning point
did not see all I had seen
time swallowed everything

I was returning home
a powerful beam guided me
was in a trance,
floating on the wings
of freedom
in the bliss of no return

Celestial Vicinity

Primordial Aum sounds in the ear
strikes and echoes in the brain cells
provokes a stream of thoughts
grey cells analyze the resonate
maps the vibrato in a digital form
tongue enchanted a name on it
hands shaped it aesthetically
fire of words spread from person to person
the wind breathed life into it, and hands felt it.
Goosebumps aroused on the skin
the fire of words spread on earth
melody of life sprang with divinity
the aroma of grace showered as rain
I meditate shutting my five senses
I am dreaming and scribbling this poem
from the celestial vicinity of the sixth sense

My Tiny Step

I find each word a poem
each person a poet
every object
an image, simile
metaphor and metonymy
on highway
ridden by great ones
I place my tiny step.

Sixth Sense

The power centres of the body are six called 'Chakras'
rise and fall of power in centres cause ill health
six qualities make life easier in this world like,
wealth, grace, knowledge, wisdom, fame, and penance
six powerful nations control the power balance of the world
shut down all your five senses, you will get a unique sixth sense

Crown of Wisdom

A new star of hope was born
in the cradle of civilization
a smile of God had lit the face of Mary
a piece of heaven fell on the earth for peace
he guided the chaotic minds to his sermon
and to the hill of Nazareth
where he conceived the Ten Commandments
he placed his mind on each soul
lit all human minds with a new delight,
solace and serenity of prayers
he helped carry his cross for his crucifixion
send a parting smile to Judas
for his kissing betrayal
he took the nails of human sins
bearing the pain and flowing his blood of love
he wore the thorny crown of wisdom
resurrected to announce a new era
of harmony and sacrifice for human values

Talk of the Town

Glamour graced in a drizzle
lifting the veil of celestial mist
she glided down to the floor of life
she was swinging in a swing
singing a song sprinkling love
her elegance became a melody
filling the minds of her fans

she entered silently into each one
leading her soft footfall to magic
she drew pictures with her steps
creating and breaking idols
spreading splendour she moved around
rousing men under her charm
she became a princess of the dream
riding a chariot of passion
tickling the minds she waved
cheering the crowd in waiting
to become the talk of the town

Love You, My Lady

They get inspired on a float
tongue twisted and silent
intoxicated in the memory of life
they roam in search of a thrill

true life that is playing havoc
first, drink on the rocks they rock
wake up the muse in deep slumber
he consumes many; drenching his soul

at last, she rises into a full bloom
an elegant moon sprinkles 'moony' shower
brings down his breathing images
in the light of his cigarette, he scribbles

his fingers shiver in ecstasy
his goddess dances in front of him
he sketches her with similes and images
some turn surrealistic capture

helplessness disturbs his thoughts
frustrated he throws away his glass
yet she dances outside on each bit of glass
he takes a sharp piece and scribbles
on his chest I Love you, my lady!

Of She

Calm sea
wave
curves move
in rhythmic
pulses
move with
deep sighs
surfer's
fondle ignite
wildfire,
ecstatic lust

Let Them Sleep in Peace

Magic cones
on desert
Great wonder
ever created
by man.
Awesome
architecture
trigonometric

Tear and sweat
of those hungry
slaves
still talks
silently.
Mighty Pharaohs sleep tight
on the dead
bones
of those
mighty men

Let me drop
a tear or two
for their souls

Let them sleep
in peace.

The Abundance

Nature is so bare and fair
displays all she got to play and play
She dances nude in the rain,
a wild rain dances for fertile soil.
invokes life into her womb.
Fresh sprouts of healthy seeds.
Melons, carrots, and snake gourds
all form part of her dreams.
She loves her apples and peaches.
Often grows the tomato on her cheeks.
When you are in your natural
she embraces you to feel her breathe.
Only human animals are dressed
with a low-cut neckline and so on.
The abundance of the earth is felt
when your body meets the raw.
She looks at your dimple and smiles.
Tells you to merge in the wilderness
of her beauty and listen to divinity.
Become part of her entity, in your birthday suits

Greed is Ruling

We are just
self-detonators
digging into
tranquil and serenity.
Prostituting
pulchritude of nature.

Greed is ruling
Crave is the culture.
Learn to
live with nature
Belong to
nature.
Respect this
earth who
feeds
lifeblood.

Just limit
the wants
we will be better off.
Live and let live.
See a flower
bloom
the saturated
beauty in it.

watch the sun
moon and stars
and vast
azure sky.
Don't you
feel
you are
a tiny spec
of an atom
in the cosmic
dream.

The magician
is playing a trick
on you

can you resist
any of the
five elements?

Waiting for the Sunshine

A Soliloquy
in a chat with pathetic fallacy
weeping mind
stretches out of the window
gets drenched
in the rain.

It is not for
the crown and throne
it's about the mundane
routine drought-stricken
mind
that makes one
to hold an umbrella.
Protection from the
severity
of cold winds, hurricanes,
and tempest.
Before deluge strikes
let me be alone and aloof
to feel me closer.
Crestfallen
I am waiting for the sunshine.

Aesthetic Purity

Off the cliff, I fell.
Rolled down the mountain range.
Settled down in a forest.
I was a hard boulder,
a tough rock to crack,
with a stone face!
Millions of years spent
in oblivion, in the obscurity
feeding through time,
witnessing
harsh seasons.
No one made a mark
on me.
Spring did not sprout
a flower bud
in my heart.

Then one day
a man arrived
with hammer and chisel.
He knocked and tuned
listened to my heart.
He said there are
seven tonnes in me.
My body got excited.

He was the sculptor
who declared

I am a man-woman rock.
He carved a piece
of me
carried to his workshop.

He spent the whole night
and day.
Slept on me when tired.
Slowly I was taking shape
the pain did not matter to me anymore.
I became clay in his hands.
turning into a half man
and half-woman.
The concept of lord shiva.
Adam and Eve.
A beauty of his concept.
He was invoking
nature and man into
a rough rock,
tuning and chipping
a seventh symphony
of sculpture.
Cutting the last flint out
he breathed life into
my soul.
I turned into
an exotic statue of his
imagination.
Still, I live in the
Golden Temple
of my mind
sanctified as an idol
of aesthetic purity.

Van Gogh in My Garden

I planted a seed
unaware of what it is
It sprouted
out of sheer grace.
A fine seedling
from my thoughts.
It grew
into a sapling.
I nurtured it
with a fertile mind,
watered with emotions.

It grew and grew
in my garden of Eden.
went through
rainy season
winter and summer.
When spring arrived
it showed
it's enthusiasm.
Some more healthy buds
leapt out of its heart.

My heart rejoiced.
One fine morning
my sober dreams
woke me up
from a snoring sleep.

The sun had
already at his desk.
I went to my garden
of images.
Oh, surprise! surprise!
there was the sun
bloom in my garden.
A sunflower
so elegantly yellow
and fresh.

Here I found
my muse
watering my mind
and Van Gogh
in my garden
painting his sunflower.

Queen of the Desert

An insignificant grain of sand
reaches as food,
consumed by the oyster.

Fate turned me into the
waves of graceful mercy.
I did penance in the belly
of time,
concealing in the shell
for a long time.

I was in the total darkness
of ignorance.
The light did not penetrate
the membrane of my obscurity.
The oceanic simulations
did not reach my senses.
Turning in myself into the
hands of unknown
I went down to the
depth of awareness.
Then one day
I found surrounded
by a rare glow.
rolling myself
in ecstasy as a pearl!

Some diver
found me.
Now I am kept
in the naval prestige
to invoke Sun rays
for the queen of the desert

A Scoop of Ice Cream

I am still crying about that
sweet cotton candy and a lollipop.
That was lost in my childhood
I got many sweet
mouth-watering Toblerone.
Lately, I found pleasure in my pain
and pain in my pleasure.
When I stretch my legs to the mystery
of life unknown, It melts like a scoop
of ice cream!
you ate it but did not.
in the process of licking your cream
if you bite your tongue you got the message!
Pain and sorrow follow the pleasure

A Verse of My Feelings

Oh my God
The door locked
I am looking for
a place to live.
Hibernate.
I am an immigrant
looking for asylum
in the poetry garden.
My husband is on the way
I came shortcut.
He took the long route.

Let me collect twigs
of words
Create a cosy nest
with ornate soft syllables.
I love to rest on a bed
of silky thoughts.
Doors decorated with
spring flowers
of an artistic pen.
At the door when I watch
the sun, moon and stars
in the vast sky
I wish to have an aesthetic
the mind of a poet.

I want my dream
filled night
with flowing images.

Let my precious
eggs are covered
with the warmth of
noble mind.
I wait for my husband
for a tight hug
with love flowing
out of a pen of
passion.
I love to dream in a simile
in comprehendible
for an ordinary mind.
I want my babies
see the world
with the effulgence
of poetic wisdom,
filled with
eternal knowledge.

Oh, my dear poet,
give me asylum
from dark clouds
hanging over the sky.
In a verse
of my feelings

Shore of Compassion

In the magnitude of
solitude,
placidity meditates.
Mind unaware
stretches to afloat
in the waveless
sea of tranquillity.

A ripple, a murmur
create waves of
distortion on shores
of mind.

I just want to
sit on this shore
of compassion
get intoxicated
in the calmness of
graceful silence.

Let me say a prayer
for the blooming
a flower of Love
in each mind!

History of Pain

History of pain.
Burdens
The sounding of springs,
creaking horror,
happiness
despair
pain and pleasure
moans
ecstasy of lust.
Late hours fixed
on Tv screen

Oh knee arthritis
diseases
deceased
wayward thoughts.
Silent weeping
fallen dreams
I have a history of
litter underneath
Each object has a memory.
Now
a fresh start
again with a new
couch

She is Dreaming

Micro womanhood of nature
taking a bath in a pool of wonder.
She just saw her ravishing beauty
reflected in the water mirror.

Her imaginary man is peeping
she had not seen a man so closer.
Awestruck her shy face smiled
retreating to the heaven of her dreams.

Soliloquy With Self

imagination is a notion
that flowers from the depth
of heart and mind.
Magic is created by
Soliloquy.
dialogue with self.
A selfie
with thrill and ambition.
Your sleep takes a snap.
Brain wrecks with ideas
puts in a word processor.
The motherboard works
over time,
comes out with a formula
maybe E=mc2!
an einstein in the making.
A brief history time
Stephen Hawking smiles.

Sometimes a rebirth
of Vedavyasa
or Shakespearian
dramatism.

Whatever imagination is
a flowering of
human brain
it spreads the fragrance
of love for humanity.

A Drop of Ambrosia

I was born a pearly dew
on a rose petal of love.
Was just a tiny spec of grandeur
glowing through a ray of hope.

I became the very transparency
of mighty benevolent nature.
The entire azure sky delved into me
as a tiny molecule of the galaxy.

Often I danced to the tune
of a subtle cosmic rhythm.
Although a drop of ambrosia
I live to invoke the purity of a baby.

I like to be a beautiful thought
a drop of honey on the lips of a child.
I like to be an ice cube reflecting,
refracting the divine rays of love.

I meditate on the beauty of the lord
listing to the yodelling music of his flute
I just love to remain on the shore of allure
with wide open innocent eyes of ecstasy

 Soul of the Tree

The soul of the tree
invoked
by the arrival of spring.
The tree flowered.
A fine fragrant
honey, full flower!

Wedding Today

When we met by words of verses
I never knew we opened a fine channel,
tuned finely to the depth of our souls.
We found a red-carpeted reception.

We saluted each other with enchants,
tried to explore our minds in length.
I found your pulchritude embracing me.
I became a slave of my emotions for you,
anxious to meet you in person.

We had our dates under moonlit,
finding the silky softness of your heart.
The more we depart each day
The more I wished to meet you soon.

I made long prayers for you
want you as my princess of dreams,
to carry you to the ecstasy of love
make you happy every moment we live.

I just have erected a beautiful palace,
There we live as husband and wife.
We make our life more worthy
by bringing our offspring into this world.
I love to be with you ever after
when we celebrate our heavenly wedding today

To Be With Marbles

I had a collection of marble
I kept it as a sacred possession
in my shoebox memorabilia.
The crystal marble had a touch of paint
few had a blue tinge like a piece of the sky inside!
had red roses blown inside for a couple
they had bubbles shining inside.
It was a like little world in
some glowed rainbow.
So had the freshness of light.
when I kept it outside under the sun
it had conceived the sun
with golden beams dancing in.
I used to roll them on my desk
for the fun of it.
Many marbles had a hit-and-rub story
They struck my knuckles
as a punishment when
I lost the marble game.
They also hit my friend's hands too.
At this age too it brings nostalgia.
I often become young to roll
with round balls of time!

Nothing but the Truth

There is a thin layer
in between
Myth
truth
and illusion
in the day-to-day life.

The life is
covered
with attributes
and adornments
of power
prestige
and ego.

The Consciousness
of false identity
rules the mind.
A thin layer
of unconsciousness
divides
life and death,
life and dream.

Once
the life breaks
the mirror of myth
you will see the
naked truth
Nothing but the truth.

Orchids Bloom

Art of writing.
Begins in the mind.
Creative juice flows,
Drawing images.
Each word takes birth from the soul,
Fluttering wings of joy,
Glides to a new world,
Hovering over the sky of imagination.
I am in love with words.
Jade of thoughts dance.
Kites of imagery float.
Love percolates from the heart.
The mind flows smoothly.
Orchids bloom with,
Prayers

He is a Xavier

He has an idiotic
solution
for problems
of the world

In the Opera House of Life

I sing a song for you like Babul singers,
fiddling the lyrics on the soul as my strings.
Thoughts ring a rhyme taping the streams,
That flow from heaven as celestial dreams.
We are the folks who folk together for songs,
leaving the home for a moonwalking stream.
With idyllic lore, we create the melody of life
drawing tunes from the cosmic chant of love.
We are singers for the gods and goddesses
filling every being with a symphony on strings.
Come dear folks let us enact a drama of the lord.
A divine comedy from the core of the vocal cord.
Let our music reach heaven for the demigods to dance.
let us score together in the opera of life!

Dark Dusky Mist

Leaving the last glow
on the platform.
The train left in a huff
making a shrill whistle.
The barren track
returned into a monologue
once again.
Puffs of smoke and steam
lingers in the fog
produces a unique smell
of train

The rain continues rippling
on the station roof.
passengers faded out
one by one.
The station lights put off

She has been standing there
in the solitude
waiting for him anxiously.
Today also he did not come
she murmured herself
and disappeared into
dark dusky mist

Do Not Waste Your Tears

The Giant nature is pushed
to the wall of human greed.
Tied to the cot of infidelity.
Chained her emotions.
Her anger is thrashed
resistance quashed.
beauty is squeezed.
she is melting down her courage.
Cruel soldiers pushed her at gunpoint,
pinning her down to hell.
Now she succumbed to their desires.
flowed and burned as fire.

I just throw a cloth of love on you Mother
Oh, My dear cover yourself.
Do not cry
let me cover you with an umbrella of love.
Your tear is precious to us
Do not waste it on them
Preserve it for the world
Those fools don't know
what they were doing.

A Rivulet of Grace

I have been watching this flow of life
with amazement.
There never was a stagnation
all through the day twenty-four hours
seven days a week, years to years
she cascaded like a melody.
Seasons passed over the valley
with splendour and serenity
making her adorned with time,
decorated with fresh sprouts.

Like a mother I watched her
admiring her exquisite beauty.
she was an avalanche from the mountain tops, she jumped,
flooded the valley with her rich heritage.
fertilized the soul of the soil before becoming a fountain of love.
She turned into a waterfall of pulchritude.
Life would be lonely and charmless
if she is not flooding with grace.
I love you, my lady of the mountain!
Never desert us to dry in the desert

From the Mystic Fog

A cascade of fond memories
arrives along with the dawn
Morning is celestially beautiful
The sun is yet to rise from heaven
His golden crown just makes an appearance
among golden-capped clouds.

We used to watch the sunrise.
The clothing of nature
with all the intricacies of makeup.
The pomp and luxury of elegance.
Birds used to lift the veil of mist
The golden drapes are parted
I used to watch her face keenly
the beauty of the eastern sky was reflecting
on her face like an expression of nature.

We talked about everything under the sun
When the mountain of loneliness
shaded on my life, I remembered her
her mannerisms, she used to glide her
hand on her silky brown hair,
feeling the hands of the wind with a smile.

Breaking my monologue
I hear you whisper soothingly to my soul

I heard you saying from the mystic fog,
"Here I am, talk to me"
I look around to see you.
A flutter of wings fades out into the vast expanse

Muse Wakeup

There is a treasure trove of words
hidden in the unvisited chambers
of history.
Here live many great men of letters,
who created a universe of their thoughts
choosing each word carefully,
flowered their vision on the tree of literature.
From the great poet Vyasa to Shakespeare
to writers of the modern era Bob Dylan.
Each word they wrote was in the golden letters
Sending a Lord of the flies to the world.
as a signature tune of their aesthetics.

Time flooded through the veins of human life.
Concepts changed to new media.
We became slaves of greed.
No time to read and write.
Even bookworms have departed.
literature is sleeping in remote corners.
The grace of the muse is not gracing anymore
the deserts and dunes consuming creativity.
Now lady Mouse is sleeping
on a bed of forgotten books
Is it, not time that we wake her up
from the deep slumber?
Let her rise in us as the queen of words again!

A Bubble in the Time

I had a dream
found me growing into a giant
beyond galaxies.
My mind was too elongated.
suddenly my world shrunk.

The entire universe
got conceived
in the womb of time.
The entity of the cosmos
turned into a bubble.
The sea, rivers the solar systems
all delved into a nutshell.

I could see the
the entire world turned into
miniatures
the aeroplanes
the ships all turned into
tiny toys.
Suddenly I break off the
dream
I come to reality from
the frozen
bubble.
The entire dream
vanishes
and the world moves on with
usual business.

Gun Powder

Words are
capsules
with
gun powder
emotions
Handle
with care.
Can burn
everything
in seconds.

A Bookworm

A librarian remains as a library.
Every volume on fingertips.
At first, they join as a temporary hand
then become a part of the catalogue.
metamorphosis into a bookworm.

A lifetime is spent dusting and labelling
climbing the ladders to the shelves
Up and down the steps several times,
searching and reserving special books

She is living in the company of literature
the writers of the world assembled
In a row of magnanimity, a hall of fame.
often talks to them about her loneliness.
scans and reads every book, every word
Nothing can escape her visions.

By the time she retires must have read
almost all the books in the storehouse.
One day she walks out of a walking encyclopedia
with a parting look at the library

I Am Colourless

I have a colour wheel
that rotates
all through the time
it carries
entires galaxies along
it spins wildly
and never stops
I tried to mark
my colour on it
but
I found myself
colourless
Has the sky any colour?
No
I am colourless too

Ambrosia of Heaven

Ambrosia streams
Through the window of heaven
From infinity a small
Windows opens into mind

The entire cosmic dream
Manifest in a pool of purity
A rivulet of thoughts fills
The mind with pure joy

Just do not want to lose
The priceless charity of nature for
Anything in the world.
I meditate on the lap of compassion

Evolve and emerge as a tiny
Drop let on a petal of a flower.
Just let me have a drop of
Celestial ecstasy in the mundane life

Guide me into the magnanimity of
Serene silence of heaven's.
Let me live here as incense
Spreading the divine fragrance of love.

See You if I Come Back

Nowadays any moment
he can ring the doorbell.
spiders are extensively spun
weaving a thread
all around the world.
Faces covered in blacks
smashes everything on the way.

The very human face is
melting down
dripping images
men and women
have cobwebbed faces.
Can see their fearful smile
Arachnophobia
is hitting the world
arachnids
roam in the world
burning to loot.

Anybody can be at the door
the government man
Police, the tax man
terrorist
fanatics.

are we living as humans
or slaves?
living every moment in fear psychosis
I think the doorbell rings
see you if I come back.

Into Daylight of Freedom

And there hides
in a flower bud
a lot of mystery.
The World has not
seen it in full.

Silky soft petals
sleep with folded
eyelids.
A dream lives
inside your eyes
in colours of life.

The exotic hue
of rainbow
still bright on
the horizon.

First ray
of the sun
tickles your body.
Slowly the
petals of life
into full bloom.

Eyes open
to the brilliance
of dawn.
fresh dew drops off
your soul
emits
the fragrance of life.

You are into
the daylight
of freedom!

Cute Smile

It is a silent talk in my silence
My thoughts are flowered at the dawn
Of imagination
Mind moves into a trance.
Slowly from the depths words stream
Ideas, imagery images and smiles flood
Through a celestial vocabulary.
Muse smiles exotically
The poet copies her elegance in words
A poem is born from the pregnancy of words.
She makes her presence with a cute smile.

Sugar

Sweetness exists
if there is sourness
Earth of sugar
would be tasteless

one has to know
all tastes to realize
the merits of sugar

the multi-faceted world
makes life sweeter
the good, bad and ugly
co-exists in life

when rain comes
sugar melts
when the sun arrives
it shall become caramel
at the winter
we will have a ball
of ice cream

that is why
lord is colourless
tasteless
shapeless

he is the
concentrated
sugar of bliss

to know him
as sweetness
one has to test
all tastes
the changeless
big granule
of sugar!

Waiting For

No, I am not looking for anything
But I like the challenge
to test my words that may tickle
sensitive, feeling fulfilling
the fragrance of my thoughts
through words of my heart
dipped in the loving sentiments

Words bloom for you on the dry
twigs of my imagination
the spring season will arrive soon
spreading the arrival of the freshness

I leave my hope with a high spirit of love
my signature tune is in the air
birds sing it loudly a symphony
the entire ambience turns choir full

I retreat into the mystery of my
unknown emotions
waiting for the lady of love!
lifting the veil of mist!

Just Some Thoughts

She washed away all the sediments
Of thoughts about him
Yet he is hanging on
With a lingering mischievous look
The infectious smile still makes waves
In her composture
Restless she waded into the depth
Of unknown pleasure
Every cell of her body heaved
In exciting memories
Ecstatic convulsions turned
her into swinging singing bird
She flew over experiencing
heavenly drizzle of love
drenching her mind with completeness

She slept dreaming of her prince of night
Over the window sill, he was resting
cuddled bleeding lips
the ocean waves had the Scarlet
emotions!

Who Am I?

I am being transported
into a tunnel
my memory takes a deep
breath
a deep dive into the
mystery of life

the soul has trekked a long way
from the endless beginning
and beginningless end

is it a collider
where they collided
a divine molecule?

I am on that endless journey
to nowhere
My mind depicts
flashes of my thoughts
my imagination
my life's blueprint

it splashes and flashes
in psychedelic colour
images dance and rattle

my stream of images
my imagery

I don't know
when this will end
the laser display
of my biological map
is it brain mapping?
who am I?
my enquiry begins here

Embers

Slowly spark
lits
bonfire
it sweeps the
twigs
smiles
to all around

the darkness
retreat
song on the
lips around
now moths
circle
warmth
flow from the lips of
red embers

If my thoughts are real?
My words turn stale
meaningless to describe you
as you are beyond
meanings, shapes and sounds
yet I try to string you
in a capsule of worthless sounds

You are a flow of the subtle song
streaming into the depth of awareness
Often making an experience of bliss
the music in between life and death
as you sing it becomes real

you are sleeping
in the petals of a dream
sleepwalks
into an exotic world
of fantasy
dances through the souls
stare through the eyes
of a curious child
You become
princess of nature

donning the gown
of colourful corollas
the lady strolls
into the wide world
each sound reverberate
from the heart of love
you are in it
delving as a divine queen
making the world sleep
in your lap of timelessness
Just sing for me alone once
caress my hair
fondle my thoughts
make me sleep in the cradle
of your lullaby

I just saw you dancing
with wolfs
grinding stars and the moon
your gown was
twinkling with stardust
then I saw you floating
with the dead moon
and stars
holding hands of embrace
muse sings to you.

Join the Mob

Whatever the colour
it is all sourced out of
one origin
joins in the
grip
of one powerful
hand

the colourless
palm
of universal love

as the stubs
reach
the caring fingers
it is ready for
further journey
into life again

sharpened
with a mission
for service
join the mob

Blanket of Ecstasy

When I saw you for real
you were undressing my fantasy
unfolding my lusty desires
I wished to become your slave
discarding my donning one by one
was unveiling your dream

my tattoos were in conversation
with your's
they embraced to cuddle in a bliss
we danced all night under moonlit
of our thrills

hugging in our birthday suits
mended your clothes of bare skin
with a needle of invisible desires
and we made the dawn to sleep
under our blanket of ecstasy

A Beautiful Lull

I just want nothing
from you
but I want you close
close to mind, soul
and body

In our silence
we learn about
our reticence
volumes we speak
merely looking
into eyes
touching with our
long sighs

our breath foment
our fantasies
With a smile, we talk
our desire
caress our lust
in our beautiful
thoughts
embrace our deepest
respect for each other

even if part
temporarily
we make a solemn promise
to meet the next day
witness
the stillness of stars
smiling moon
hot sun
the rhythm of the earth
the mystery of the night

under the cover of
night
I meet
hugging our
bodies
feeling the aromatic
smell of
virginity

we never possess
each other
yet we tag
on to our love
infinitely

Love is
a beautiful lull

A Drop of Ambrosia

a drop of ambrosia
from heaven
on an exotic petal of a dream
with all elegance
she was invoked
incarnated
an angelic beauty

inhaled the freshness
of mother nature
awestruck
with wide-open eyes
she conceived
the entire galaxies
with a wink
floated on her wings
carrying a myth
the secret of creation

The Idol

made you a lovely clay lump
kneading caressing
fondling emotions
created you, carved you
with magic hands
invoked grace on the lips
painted naked colours
adorned with my
aesthetic sense
decorated with love
ultimately smashed
the idol of my lust

Lost His Entity

Once when stripes of time
was with him
wearing a suit of arrogance
the attire of an intoxicant youth
who thrashed the earth
wished to
crush everything on earth
he had a hat of hubris
with a feather on it
one day another challenger came
he lost his entity
hat too

Avalanche

Angry Blue Mountain range
slides as the glacier
runs over everything
grabbing rare moments of the play
a maniac on a destruction spree

attracted by the rare valley of flowers
he came down to settle
in the shade of calmness
I write these line
witnessing the avalanche

Ditch me to fate
Were you not
building
a fence around you
all through
the years
of infidelity?

by the time
you became
alienated
covering yourself
in the tattoo

of animated
animals
who were
ready to pounce
at me
from parts
that you
kept away
from me

now he
took over
while you
ditch
me
to fate

Earthly Songs

Harping on the strings
of mind
soul gets invoked

lyrics flower
in the thoughts
as words of
wisdom
an incessant
stream of
divinity
in the form of
music
rejuvenates
the dry plateaus
sprouts the
springs of earthly
songs

My Contradiction Invokes

My contradiction invokes
myself
I negate everything in search
of something
I have to find out
Yet to know what it is
then one day
I shredded my mind,
the weight of ego
my anger, my frustration,
I found myself
hiding close to my heart
A smile bloomed on my lips
I could not
subtract me
Because I am what I am
how can I contradict
my entity?

Your Dream Again

The invigorating smell of your mother
intoxicates my soul
let me roll on your body
imbibe the aromatic nectar of life
from the breasts of your compassion

I listen to your heartbeat
can hear the entire beings ticking in your heart
the symphony of your love

I am dreaming suckling tasting
the ambrosia of your love

many came to this earth
invoked by the grace of your wishes
all returned to you as dust

some placed their signature in your heart
turned into the salt of you
they were the great men who
became your pride
the diamonds who sent out
the beams of hope and gratitude

we erected our empires, nations,
cutting you into sizes.
stampeded on you, crushing

we thought we ruled over you
did we?
who did own you? none
all have left

the cruel rulers, kings and queens
dictators, conquerors,
yet you lie with a smile

your womb giving fresh breath for animations
silky sprouts of vegetation
let me salute you my mother and pray
to be born again and again
as a child of your soulful creation.
Your dream again!

The Veins of Sweet Wilderness

A great sculptured
posture
chiselled out of
flesh and blood
by the great composer

the rhythm of
ecstasy
flows through
the veins of
sweet wilderness

each nerve string
sings a melody
of the nude
blissful embrace

To the Warmth of Love

They meet
under a spontaneous
feeling
two lips
tuned lips(tulips?)
chat in subtle senses
nothing they say
just
feel the fire
foment the rhythm

the burning wishes
touch
the silky warmth
on the orange anthers
suck the saliva
of desires

meet the tounges
in flame
they just want nothing
but to burn
themselves

forget the
world
and hug tight
to the warmth of love

Your Kingdom

Yes we can
say one prayer daily at dawn
nothing just say
make me you in me
me in you
sweep the mind away
say
oh lord I am the only
the bad person in this world
make me a good being
of love
help me
feel good about others
let me tie
all the wandering
animals
the beasts
in my mind
eliminate my mindless mind
live and let live
all beings and non-beings
yes we can do that for you
that is your envisaged kingdom!

Master Planner

Praying hands to touch
the heart of the lord
prayer songs melt him down
drizzling his grace

fertilises the rough
unploughed soil
tills the land and
plants a seed of love
looks after, wedding
watering enough
raining at times,
protects with a fence
turns himself as
scarecrow
day and night vigil

sent seasons
to see his plants
bloom
bear fruits of his love
makes sure
nothing is left out
off his plan
the master planner
of the universe!

My busted bubble
carry you in a palanquin
of my imagery
your rhythmic tilting body
eyes wide with awe

a silky veil of shyness
dangle in your eyes
thousands of dreaming stars
adore the azure sky

your long blue-black hair
caressing the breeze
flints of the shining beams of light
dance in your dimples
the moon just kisses your forehead
drizzling aromatic mists
your every move elegant
like the soft feathers of a swan

I live in the bubble of a dream
aware of inevitable
my busted bubble
lie scattered

A New Vision

Evening sun
just dived into the western sea
taking a bloodbath
washing away the murder of the day
soon dusk will dawn
seeping darkness into the world
angelic birds return home
a hard day's toil

harping a monotone
night arrives
thoughts of the day
arrive like bats
settles hanging upside down
on branches of life

tweaking louder and louder
streaking sins of the day
sounds evening prayers
before the altar
in the dim candlelight

red eyes glow
piercing the night

they all meet in a congregation
saying their prayers all night
invoking angels
and return to the dawn

wings stretched they move
echoing to eternity
echolocating lost souls
filling with a new vision
until dusk falls back
to dark ego

Stanza 2

Children's bodies wither
shadows spread
wet teardrops fall salted
hunger bred;
sounds of growls in tummies
ride a breeze.
No beds or bread,
crawling on scarred knees.

voracity for a handful of anything
to put out the fire of ravenous
she crawled under camouflage
hands stretched for food in the form of a god

My Anger

the power cut off yesterday
sweat pours worked overtime
cursing and swearing
night disappeared
for a dawn of mishaps

the milkman did not come
the morning started with black tea
the usual newspaper came late
same power failure

the stomach is filled with anger
bubbles of an upset
on the front page the owlish face
of the leader
with a gesture to the opposition leader
anger floods everywhere
insufficiency of governance

parliament in pandemonium
exhibition of hegemony in the legislature
they squat to discuss
how to increase their salary and benefits

in the tv channels
his dummy pop show
meeting with presidents and prime ministers
teaching the techniques
how to laugh at the miseries of the people

eliminated truncated judiciary
one last laugh
I laughed my anger away
Democratic hypocrisy
survives everywhere
ha ha ha

Viewing Deep

viewing deep
the depth of silence
carries you into mystifying
mystery of mind
there hides a treasure trove
unexplored unearthed
suspense of unknown
remains of past
fossiled in between
past and future

the pendulum of the mind swings
back and forth
in search of tranquillity
when the momentum stops
to the silence of happiness
pleasure thrusts

canvas in the easel
hand and brush moves
uncontrolled
celestial
strokes create an artifice
a snap of a finger

chin rests on the palm
wondering
who created the Biennale
I walk
under moonlight
adding a picture of my long shadow
slow motion

The Darkness of Night Recedes

The darkness of night recedes
to the backdrop of his beautiful smile
cool breeze flow caressing everyone
bundle of puffy white clouds scatter
star-studded azure sky glace the lake
mind floats with the waves
sounds of silver anklets of Trinkle
thoughts flow incessantly
there is nothing beautiful as the moonlit night
living images of dreams wander
breathing the fragrance of jasmine
beauty pervades through
delved deep into meditation
I see his reflection in the lake
like the flow of the milky way to earth
my eyes closed invoking the divine mother
sitting on a throne on the moon
Oh, mother let me worship you with these words

Visions From Life

All that he had seen started to grow in him
the colours and scenes, life sketches, caricatures
events of installations, memories, lifestyles
emotions experience, passion, love, dreams

all he painted with his mind
his thoughts grew in the palette mixing pixels
spreading lights and shades into his body, mind and spirit

like a performing artist, he existed in a trance
with hue and pigments from the previous life

his visions took the breath from the past
carving his body, he sculptured and chopped off his desires
until he became a perfect theme for his canvas
becoming himself a unique painting for generations to see

Still Thirsty

how one can possess
an illusion in delusion
In a dream, I am a king
possessing the entire world
ruling the subjects

wearing a crown of jewels
jewellery all over my body
diamond studded swords
all fine objects

then descending
falls from the dream
waking up to the reality
becoming a pauper
wearing rags
begging for alms
where have all fine things gone?
all vanished
falling for a belly dancing
tempting mirage
still thirsty

My Teardrops Weep Silently

from the hangover of yesterday
I was hanging on a delicate thread
between delusion and reality
eyes were half closed unable to open eyelids

yet, your silent shoe flower footfall
woke me up smelling your fragrance
you had already entangled me
with a stringless passionate knot so tight

saw your image everywhere
in all beings and non-beings
with a sigh of my breath, I inhaled you
into the depth of my unlimited cravings

chanted your name in my each breathe
worshipped invoking your idol of ideals
dreamed you each moment
cried silently when I could not remember the second
you lost in my thoughts and vision

my teardrops weep silently for your touch
you became half of body and spirit
embracing the platonic attachment
we loved turning into one reality, one universal love

Lotus

Every time I see her
she gives me a subtle smile
among the luxuriant green valley
see her body cuddled
like a folded palm in prayers
a pink goblet upside down

I smile at her sending the first rays of hope
a message of love through messenger clouds
she opens her lotus eyes slowly
still, dreaming from remnants of last night
her silky pink petals open
cascading dew of the dawn
drizzling a dazzling smile scattering globules
shyness shadows her beauty
making it glow in the golden litter I send her

with a fine warm kiss, invoke her enigma
she wades a little in the water
avoiding a beetle
as a lovely message she sends
her mysterious aroma in the breeze
I embrace her until the nightfall
and return into the depth of intoxication
into the ocean of ravishment until the next sunrise
when I see her float in full pink bloom
where lotus feet of muse dance

The Fish Skeleton

this year the summer is sultry the sun is looking stern with a thousand
eyes melting down gold nuggets into a stream of liquid metal.
the entire earth turning into red hot, airless stuffy stifling rooms
waterholes barren, where the mirage lives. he stretched his hands to
caress a lotus, she became a pinch of ash

the fish skeleton
remnants of the last supper
shines under the sun

Until I Merge (Obsession)

along the path, we had a close
remote umbilical cord connection
from a high-raised pedestal of love
we met transcending the unreal

meditated in the thoughts of each other
invoking the freedom of truth
the warmth of our embrace reduced
us to the oneness of passionate compassion

ecstatic walk holding the stalk of eternity
we missed ourselves in the mystery of God
I could hear your whisper everywhere
teasing me with the primordial sound
in the sea and waves, the breeze,
the sunlight and moonlight
every grain of sand, in every being and non-being
I was madly in love

but I could not see your bodily presence
yet you were near and far
did I possess you at all?
how could I?

you were in a hide-and-seek game
from the depth of my imagination
realms of my obsession
reached here on this cliff of no return

ready to tumble down in search of your echo
maybe I would catch you up
delving into a tunnel of brilliance
where you live like a queen of my image
will not leave you until I merge in the flame of eternity
losing myself in a psychedelic trance
inducted by the chant of your thousand names

Waiting for None

the train moves fast
nothing escapes from the shadow of time
the reality of a hegemony
is very much in a show
together we trekked
many lands
visited far and wide
mountains and seashores
breathed air
placed our imprint
ate and drank
possessed and dispossessed

hand in hand
we painted our life together
in a train, we are all co-passengers
travelling to unknown destinations
yet we met
lived in a short span of the journey
exchanged pleasantries
tried to live in a compartment
visualising our stations to arrive

many sceneries and scenarios
pass past the cabin windows
eyes catch

a procession of mourners
body covered in a red silk
carried by pallbearers
dry faces embedded in sorrow
soon the body will be ashes

each one gets down
at one station or the other
the train will continue its run
waiting for none

Slicks on the Shore

Doomed in the depth
submerged in the abyss of the ocean floor
I rot corroded
daily the sun emerges from the coral reefs
with a broad spectrum of smile
he wakes me up

once I was sailing through
the seven seas
carrying a lot of egoistic
egocentric cargoes
thinking it as precious
diamonds, gold bars
revolving in a tornado
I was pushed through
whirlpool consumed my entity

flooding my weight in the flood
trapped me bleeding on a reef
Flotsam of my treasures
streaming in the sea currents
depositing on continent's
as Jetsam
my throwaway crude
slick on the shores of life
wings stuck

Melody

golden silky waves of sunlight
moves in rhythmic intervals
see through summer veil
hides the masterpiece of nature
clad in exotic seasonal attires
trees shower aromatic mist
their floral gown sway in the breeze
white puffy clouds play hide and seek

snow-capped mountains melt
In trinkets of silver
tweaking little birds sings the music of the season
the azure sky reflects in the lakes and rivulets
silvery little fishes somersault

a dream unfolds before my vision
intoxicated legs stroll around
levitating in the tide of melody

Since Then

it is like magic
sitting behind wheel
igniting
hand break down
the neutral gear up
slowly accelerates
pressed pedal a little strong
the engine roar

remember the slow release of the pedal
the car moves with a jerk
memory recoups training sessions
my car moves smoothly
unnecessary horning
eyes rove on both sides
watch side walkers
side mirrors
oh it brings the whole world to view
and rearview mirror
carries in the whole of the universe inside

slowly picks up speed
change of gears
with a jerk and sounding brrrrrr.
once more the terrible face of the instructor

narrow lane
got to manoeuvre
a cyclist, oh no
how to escape unhurt
somehow leg finds the brake pedal
car stops
he passes with a funny smile
at last, escaped a big accident
decides to go further ahead
to a more busy semi highway
Yea I can drive
faster

twenty-five years passed
since my first drive
still, remember like the first day at school
just hop in
I can take you wherever you want
In my Hyundai i1o Sportz

Twig -nest

before the monsoon, it completed
grand structure for my siblings to play
I and my boyfriend meticulously built our abode
selected best fibres from all around the world
brought fine silk cotton from the forest
arranged kids bedroom
decorated with pictures of Donald, and Mickey
put small holes for ventilation

the branch we selected was unique
the first ray of the sun reached us directly
I could imagine my chicks peeping through the window to the new
world
the fragrance of mango flowers
tender mangos swing in the wind
had our home camouflaged
afraid of the rat snake and that horrible chameleon, his long destructive
tongue

my guy was happy tweaking a melody
every day at dawn
we had our dinner under moonlit

at last, the first egg came and more
we both sat on it warming it with our hopes and love
at last, that wonderful day arrived

one by one babies broke the shells
three girls and two boys
we are proud mother and father

beyond the great wall of China, I see a similar nest
it is not at all better than our little twig nest

Ballerina of Heaven

celestial mist glides down silently
the magic show unfolds with grandeur
an angel arrives with rainbow wings
awesome soft subtle music streaming

she steps into the limelight in elegant steps
ballerina steps into every heart like a dream
a story enacts in a dance drama
she lives in the arena as a warm experience

the perfection of classic dance glides in
she moves in the air swiftly in twists and turns, a heavenly dance
expressions of all seasons
spring swept in
summer warmth
picturesque autumn
winter of Bethlehem
aromatic raindrops
the years of hard work and practice on display
inspiring divine melody tap dance in every spectator
holding her soft hands with a long kiss of admiration

Off the Cliff, Why?

trekking a long way reached a cliff
a lion's review with binoculars of mind
thoughts are cliff-hanging
seventy years of journey
with a pocket full of peanuts
an unopened lunch box full

eyes wander a three-sixty circle
far away from the fields
still the faded green memory sprouts
meadows, valleys and rivulets
pastures, wild forests
many birds and animals lived with
hopes and dreams
satisfaction and dissatisfactions
happiness and sorrow
departed friends and relatives
colleagues who outsmarted
won that promotion
childhood friends,
played marbles and tops with them
girlfriends
accomplishments, failures

Then one day
Holding a walking stick
shivering legs and a sort of Parkinson's syndrome
while looking back
there remains nothing
just vague grey syndrome
there is only one hue
the old rickety life

from that end
a baby crawls toddle, a boy or girl,
then a robust young man holding a hand
the bangles
middle of life
retirement,
a person, non-entity
searching for something
what is that?
why?
Ultimately off the cliff
why?

He Is a Doyen of Liers

he is a doyen of liers
master of manipulation
running a kingdom of sycophants
selling utopia
for a price for poor innocent Americans
coined slogans
American Greatness
pride, prestige and racism
during campaign
his cronies lit a bonfire
rain danced
trapped voters
got burned their wings
clipped the voter's

from the lab of conservatives
he got himself reincarnated
Frankenstein the twenty-first
raised from the ashes
with a thirst for gulping the world
suck the blood like Dracula
slowly his victims rise from the graves
with thirsty fangs
he captures them in his charm
crucifix with the pillars of democracy

connects himself friendly with
maniacs, megalomaniacs, dictators
autocrats, mafia dons turned rulers
hides a lot of skeletons in the cupboard
exhibits with a rocking laughter

like a foolish Goliath
challenges the world
threatening world leaders
inviting a Boston tea party

all the bad crooks are his friends
pretends himself as the courageous cat
challenging everybody
selling a dream to the Americans
a dream merchant selling his dreams
no takers
some times he pisses on the street
possessed by devil
when madness turns wild
there will be a David with a stone and sling
wonder who will bell the cat

Felling the Bush

it is like a tough bush

tropical forest

to enter there cutting down the base growth

They move in slowly

add some water

smooth a little

you are ready with scissors

hear the soft and rhythmic sound

cut cut cut

I often wonder how the hairdressers

make that sound with scissors

some barbers enter mercilessly

with a sharp knife

after applying foam lavishly

it gives the fine smell of old spice

he starts gliding his knife

smoothing swashing the hair

wipes it on his forearm

slowly a portion of the forest cleared

and move down to the neck

here one has to be cautious

God knows when he may ask for a ransom

now the growth is felled
white skin shines
the sun penetrates unseen land
now the stylist is designing sideburns
carved a fine moustache
he applies aftershave lotion
a musk smell spreads in the air
applies snow and medicated
talcum powder

That Is It

cloth cover around the neck removed
moonlit face
a soft confident smile

Chiming Words

each word an angel
floats on the wings of thoughts
when an idea strikes mind reacts
fishing for the right expressions
the hidden sounds flow
syllables and slang in the throat
steps out on the ramp
walking up and down the tongue
finely worded melody
rap, classical singing

conversation, a small talk
lovelorn tongue-tied
firebrand speech
speak of fire in the vocabulary
enough to inflame a mob
revolutions come through the mouth

subtle soft flute music
that conveys a flow of soulfulness
early morning symphony of birds
trumping seagulls
melodious bluebirds
crowding ravens
morning chant of hymns by sages
may there be peace and harmony

in thoughts, words and action
be my words as flowers at the feet of nature
let it float like a Lotus
so beautiful

Nine Facial Expressions

Invoked by the spirits
slowly she walked in
her petal feet gliding
possessed by holy angels

ballerina from heaven
arrived behind a veil of mist
a ceremonial dance is in the offing
thick smoke rises from the sacrificial hearth
smell of incense
mystery mystic hangover

vibrant drumming
behind the smock screen, she comes out
colourful crown made of fresh palm leaves
on her head
the moon shows his face

every move each step carefully
her colourful costumes change
like a peacock, she dances
soft bluish-green quills move with the rhythm

dances of world
visited in her
Indian classical, Katha Kali
kathak, mohiniattam
Russian Ballet
Spanish flamingo
Western classical
Puppet dancing
frantic dance of shiva

nine forms of expressions
hand and finger mudras (signs)
enter her face
her mind body and intellect
interact with her body
waves of ecstatic tempo
turning herself into a divine dance
a court dancer from heaven
sprinkling sparkling exotic light beams

 Wolfs in Sheepskin

they all come in different costumes
some with a tube light in their mouth
dressed in hand-spun khadi cloth
symbol of modern hypocrisy
honey drippings in words
becoming momentary angels
weaving dreams for downtrodden
wolfs parading camouflaged in sheepskin
holding all kinds of manifestoes
promising heaven on earth
putting dirty fingers in the saltless porridge of poor
stealing the bread of others
goes away onto ivory towers soon
after getting elected

Now in power
cursing roaring
hitting the noses of freedom
rule and rule with a whip
siphoning treasury
steal our taxes without shame
go on junkets
extort by more taxes
hate democratic values
suck blood like Dracula's
fearful fangs on display when addressing the nation
Then come back with a crocodile smile again

My Dream World

from infinity, she walked in
wearing a blanket of greenery
a murmur passed through forests
breathing freshness around
she started caressing the woods

the lady had dressed in her exquisite long gown
all the coloured butterflies
camped adoring her elegant robe
her face lit with hues of a rainbow
dancing in soft steps he created
a disco floor floodlit by the sun moon and stars

the flow of rhythmic drumming
the sweet music of cosmodrome
laser beams revolving in tunes
the hiding coloured wingers flew in
the great trees embraced them
doning new silky dresses for the season
flowered dry leaves fall
worshipping the mother autumn
thrilled my ink flows into a dream world

Let Me Dream About You

May flowers bloom in the cradle of spring
the chariot from heaven arrives with an exotic bloom
in the womb of nature, a unique special baby meditates
every second the mother feels the thrill

dreams of a father and anxiety of a mother
takes shape in the depth of divinity
time passes through the channel of life
where the pieces of hearts beat rhythmically

soft petal feet toches in the belly
my child holding on to the thread of grace
praying to prepare for a celestial journey into the life
oh, my baby, the best that is happening to me

when you arrive let me arrange the best for you
the best cradle made of sandalwood
petal-like beddings
blanket you with the warmth of love
toys of nature

I sing a lullaby from the depth of love
make you sleep in my dreams
I swing the cradle all night for you
when you are hungry I keep your little stomach with my ambrosia

want to hear your first sound
then your first smile when you are full
let me carry you in my imagination
until you arrive in June
amongst drumming of the first monsoon rains
Earth wakes up enthralled with fresh sprouts.

I Listen to Her Love Beats

sediments of time
leftover daylight
giant darkness spread his wings
streaked trees display
autumnal breeze
embraces the first winter night
the murmur of cold winds
first snowflakes
flutter around the valley
I cover my face with a blanket
sleep hugs me tight to her warm breasts
lullaby
I listen to her love beats

End My Monologue

you left suddenly and walked out in a huff
closing all windows and doors
my window with a view is blocked
skyscrapers sprung around
obstructing sun and moonlight
stars used to peep into our bedroom

pouring blue lights
pieces of snow clouds visited us
our dreams were colourful
like the dancing butterflies
during spring season

I loved watching your dark blue hair
flutter behind your neck
your moonlit blossoms
your booms shine
depth of your dimples, slightly parted lips
made me dive into you
explore fathoms of inner currents

we flew over
above the magic lands
fantasy islands where we nested
our dreams
erected magic arch of a rainbow
weaved many silky thoughts together

yet, you left dumping our home
into the hands of loneliness
making a dustbin

still, I wait for you
for the memorable day
you arrive to light the fire
spread the warmth of your laughter
your giggle, smile
let us light that oil wick
in the brass sacred lamp

I am tired of soliloquy
end my monologue, Please

A New World

after a long time, I am seeing him daily
he has changed a lot from my childhood days
now with piercing eyes, red, stern, angry rays
changed his hairstyle like a spread of noodles
and side-trimmed crew cut

my daughter too, seeing him daily with me at dawn
our audience lasts until he rises from his water bed
lately, he has been sober, compassionate, graceful too
by one go he confined all humans into their homes
sending little suns corona

now mother earth relaxing in a smog-free abode
fresh air, water, serene azure sky, new sprouts
exotic bloom of flowers silky leaves, green trees,
no forest fires, no aeroplanes anymore; all grounded,
ships do not sail, motorcars sitting rusted in the garages,

dumping of wastes in the sea, no more
factories closed, no pumping of factory wastes to the sea
very little carbon dioxide in the air, carbon monoxide
neither sulfuric rainstorms nor depletion of the ozone layer
ultraviolet radiation, negative

vacation for the killing of animals for meat,
culling of chickens stopped
delicacies for the dinner tables
are not cooked, no steaks, barbecue parties

temperature reduced, no sunstrokes anymore
the ocean is happy and sends her happy tidal waves
all the rivers to flow peacefully, earth sleeps silently
under moonlight nights, stars dance blissfully

flowers bloom to a Newfoundland
playing with the breeze sending fragrance to all corners
bees, butterflies, and beetles visit often
enjoying pollen and nectar

cosmic music and rhythmic nature synchronizes
a whole lot of multicoloured birds visit
they sing a symphony of peace and harmony
the morning theatre is in full swing
as devils are quarantined in sanatoriums

my daughter runs out
with her little steps to a new world order

Mother Hen

half boiled egg
just broke split
yolk flows sideways
embryo red streaming
in the plate
touches the wheat bread
slices forming a pool

the steam
fine smell of sulphur dioxide
some times
I see two hot bull eye
staring at me

on the side
hot lava getting cooled
forming
volcanic rock
mixing with my cornflakes

at last
the hot lava
settles in the hungry bowels
the earth table shifts
just to balance
equilibrium

don't you see
the angry red eye
of nature
tectonic
the mother hen

With Your Magic Eyes

here is my dream bottled in words
I set sail my hopes to reaching you a surprise

each letter was carved from the depth of my thoughts
erected a mansion adorned with selected
artefacts

don't know when you will find it
maybe trade winds carry it up to you
I have wrapped it with my imagination
sometimes a sailor will fetch it to you
maybe a fisherman will give you
inside a fish you bought
a sea wave shall carry it In her lap
place it on the shore as a surprise present
when you were in anguishing with a pathos song
you only will find it with your magic eyes
I am sure

My First Train Journey

my first train journey
a boy of twelve visiting a nearby town
to see a friend
always railway stations
give a sort of pleasure and pain

the station was crowded
many inward trains arrive
express train departs
waving hands of parting
likes the smell and sounds of platforms
hawkers, food vendors,
coffee boys, newspaper trolleys
their peculiarly tuned tones
In those days there was no electric
or diesel locomotives
most of the trains run on steam engines
using coal as fuel

being a passenger train
It stops at all stations
have to travel about two hours
to reach my destination
sultry heat
perspiration wetting my clothes,
the train was empty

occupying a side seat I made
I self comfortable, fan on the top
was producing crackling sounds
while disposing of hot air

heat and tiredness closed my eyes
slowly I dived into a doze
suddenly a blaring whistle an express ran past
thought my train was moving backwards
maybe clearing the way for the fast train
suddenly my train stopped
and the scenery outside remains the same

pinched on my cheek
to make sure I am not dreaming
while trying to get down
my train was moving slowly
leaving the platform saving me from a fall

Aarummula Mirror

it was an ornate gift from grandma
very prestigious privileged present
had specially mentioned in her will
an exquisitely designed mirror
known as Aarummula mirror
made with an alloy of tin and copper
polished several weeks to get the reflective surface

history of the culture and craftsmanship
of a remote village reflects in the mirror
British could not understand brilliant technology
grandpa bought the artwork at a gift shop
for grandma
priced possession she cherished

all through life, she showed looker's real self
gave confidence or false confidence too
grandma spoke to her in silence alone
complained often with hopes
glass conveyed comfort and love
talked in silence with love and compassion

time passed through reflections
no one knew the transition, transportation
however, she showed timely faces without bias
grandma spends her happiest moments looking into
slowly she knew the changes on her face
greying hair locks, wrinkles pale skin

saw faded looks
humidity haze
lazily she wrote on her image
wiped the sweating mirror
whole life in the stage
autobiographic sketches
live's pictures
end of beginning
beginning of an end

the entire universe looks like
reflection in the mirror
images really outside the glass
but inside too

grandma often visits the mirror
calls Lacy her granddaughter
tell her bedtime stories
comforts her with compassion
in the loneliness in the silenced
they danced together in thoughts
watch together the movies of the world
listen to music
Lacy sleeps embracing grandma through
the magic mirror

Photojournalists

he was there in the action
holding his digital gun
the rain did not drench his spirits
roamed with his journalistic thrills

captured every raindrop
every pathetic scene from the
rain theatre
people drenched
body mind and spirit floating
over the floodwaters
homes doomed
submerged in mud waters
cattle and pets dead afloat
decomposed flesh gapes

the entire state was flooded
western and eastern ghats
soaked in monsoon downpours
chocolate sponge cake soaked in syrup
ready to disintegrate any moment

thunderbolt and splinter of lightning roots
frantic dance of cabaret
drumming, wild music
suddenly a loud skid

mass of mountainside slides
moves faster down the forest
a lonely wild bull elephant runs
he smashes everything on his way

Victor George the journalist photographer
standing on a ridge shooting the landslide
pictured caving in row houses
settlements in the forest
the fruits of their hard labour, hardships
gilding down in muddy slides
bodies buried hands and legs mutilated
still the flow of sorrow, horror, and pain in the eyes

victor's body was found plugged
in the sticky mud pool
empathy and sorrow flowing out of his eyes
his camera still holding the scenes
for the next day's newspaper

Blood of Greed

The Ambarnaya River
goes from a greenish-brown
to crimson red where the diesel fuel is present.
she is just a young girl
turned into puberty
looking forward towards a glorious life
ahead she saw many dreams

snowcapped mountains
serene valleys
smells of different lands
flowers on her pathways

bedecked trees with a fresh bloom
archways of rainbow
aromatic mist
her eyes wide with thrills ahead

birds and animals quenched the thirst
people bathed
children played along the banks
nurtured many freshwater fishes
aquatic life
they swam in the crystalline water

with the song of September, she danced carefreely
far ahead in the town, she saw dangerous sparks
from one tunnel she was fed poison
saw criminals parading
riding horses of greed
they were cruel desperados
criminals
at a remote place

they deflowered her
near the Russian city of Norilsk in Siberia.
raped and looted her
turned her into...
dreams she had
was turned crimson
there flows her blood unnoticed

young lass would've faded behind
the iron curtain of greed
if there wasn't a guardian
secret eye to watch the hooligans

Time Too Frosted There

time too frosted there
she had never seen
the dawn since...
not even a ray of hope
sun sleeps

entire cobalt ocean
became rock blocks
underneath
another world
a full house of marine life
coral reefs

treasure troves
whales hiding from whalers

Come to the Silent Valley

come to the silent valley
forest damsel is awaiting
in her silky green grass attire
her robe decor vines theme
wild exotic flora
the emitting, soft fragrance of the forest

wholesome wildlife
rare species insects
cool spiders, centipedes
beetle in red white yellow
overcoat
uniquely designed
butterflies, wings in rainbow
virgin lassie holds a sweet smile

sprinkle sweet water
from the sudden tropical rain
the sun peeps down parting mist
white cotton clouds come behind
wrap you in silk cotton
embracing

the chirping birds
surprisingly they arrive with a melody
fluttering exhibiting their quills
in exotic colour

monkey families
children in their Sunday mischievous best
hornbills talking loudly
symphony of birds
silver owls dozing off

Mr snakes and his family
green snakes
squirrels saluting shouting
full of surprises
behind every bush and tree
long prop roots
Tarzan used to swing, fly
tall trees
nesting families

thrill magic and mystery
furls and unfurls to each visitor

Brain Cells Are Buzzed

brain cells are buzzed
with thousands of bees
hard at work unaware
signalling through motor nerves

this world is a built-up
of jigsaw puzzles
on one side the creation
the other side sustenance
third side destruction takes place

butterflies move their wings
in synchronization
sprinkling coloured dust creating graffiti images on the walls of destiny

artists, painters, and poets foresee
miraculous events of future
their words, pictures, point
a direction to the world
clear writings on the walls
farsighted predictions

each artwork is a puzzle
to be decoded
like the mystery of the infinite
from the black holes of time

Pollutants

I am just sitting on the shore
watching the magnanimity
of the great ocean of poetry
therein magnitude of the cobalt sea

her silver beaded anklets splash
giggling like an exotic elegant girl
far ahead the masters surfing
with the muse, jumping over mountainous waves

they created poetry by diving into
abyss of the marine world
harvested exotic pearls from the bottomless chasm
plucked romantic alluring corals
painted life poems in every hue on the horizon

like great rock-cut monuments of Washington
daily clouds form as busts of Shakespeare, Kalidasa, Vyasa, Dante,
Homer, Keats Shelley, Byron

I scribble my poem on the beach
quickly She stretched her feet and sweep
wiped away the pimples on the face of my muse
Pollutant eliminated

Her Silence Is Eternal

muse is silent always
silence is her essence
of all creations,
as an exponent of sixty-four art forms
she adorns this world
manifests in every atom
decorates each aspect
breaths life into
pulsating each moment
invocation wakes her up
from the meditative deep sleep

poets capture her every mood
changes attire
by a wink of her eyes
her blue-black hair reaching galaxies
adornment of golden planets
glittering diamond stars
exciting colours
an extensive palette
with all the hues and pigments
of the universe

poets, writers, painters, sculptures
singers, folklores dancers,
all at work

making her body clay
sketch books, canvas she becomes model
all that is moulded
yet to be structured are
on her torso

there is she everywhere
in the wind, ocean, sky,
Earth, water and fire
yet she is silent
with a smile on the corner of her lips

after writing on infinite pages
about her beauty
every word is scanty
her serene silence is eternal
I dream of her in every possible image

She Lives in a Thick Forest

she lives in a thick forest
a dreaming fairyland
deer leaping excitedly
drizzling rainforest of rare
species of flora and fauna
seasons arrived in successions

dreamland bloomed
exotic smile of bushes
purple, pink, marigold
pure white bunches, orchids
of all shapes and shades
idols of creatures in flora

mild fragrance
the deer her designer outfit
grew in elegance
her dreamy eyes
unfolded stories of her vision

each cell of hers
jumped out thrilling
suddenly a bushfire
the long tongues
thousands of them started licking
a towering inferno

mountain of fire
enslaving enclaving encircling
enveloping embracing
wild flames

she was barbecued
her young pink purple skin blackened
sneezing sounds blood
exploding bones
cracking skull
she turned into a glowing cinder
into ashes
breeze carrying it
sprinkling the seeds for regeneration

Sprout of Hopes

once every twelve years
those angels Strobilanthes kunthiana, kurinji visits earth in winter
light purple, winged angels
from the heavenly lavender palace

spreading light blue elegant wings
they dance to the symphony of
cosmic rhythms stepping on
earth with horseshoe flower-shaped feet
light fragrance of Yardley
From The Wood Where Spars Were Got

under the cool delight
angels dance with the wind
creating Mexico waves
in the eternal ocean of flora
flamenco dancers of the season

as the clock changes its tone
curtain for the season falls
angels losing their wings
retreats to a deep slumber
until the next cycle of hues arrive
for a fresh sprout of hopes
on the face of the wonderland earth

Last Look of the Soul

had his last breath last night
somebody closed the eyelids
life departed through the wide-open mouth
nostrils closed with cotton lumps

a dark flame in a darkened wick lamp
weeping with head down
two broken coconut hemisphere
the incense spread the aroma of death

faded wreaths with foul smell sleep on the body
soon the priests arrive, the last ceremony
covered in red silk, mourners carry the body to a pyre
leaving last hope of re-entry his aura takes a last look and departs to
eternity

Oil Slick

Thick crude oil flows from the sky
a wild drizzle of carbon granules
the day had already retreated into the ocean
covering the seven seas with slicks

the darkened face of rainbow
marine life wearing a dark robe
elegant mermaids took a swim
turned into an obsidian mannequin

seagulls gasping for breath
their wings stuck in the slick
devilish creatures glide in their wings
vultures fly high viewing the scenario

devils and demons in their Dracula robe
visits the earth screaming at odd hours
bundles of newspapers with no editorials
carbon black burned on four sides
depicting the death of democracy
the face of a bison challengingly

Just a Dust

the only rule is to have fun
the windy plains of cairns
my thrilled hopes afloat
as hot air helium balloons
an array of bulbs in different colours

windswept agri fields
lie sleeping under haystacks
the chill air was piercing
biting the skin through by wind blazer
rattling teeth
Breathe spats a spray of fog

the technicians filling the
belly of a kangaroo
with helium
it is our flight for an hour or so
slowly his belly was full

the flight pilot took his position
adjusting his gear
tuning his flame nozzle
we all aboard in the big basket
about twenty tourists
they started to explain flight procedures

soon we took off
soon we were removing
our jackets one by one
the heat was burning our skin

were gliding about three thousand
feet
below the landscape changed
tiny fields Lilliputians
small toy cars and trucks
toy boats, tankers, luxury liners
I saw floating continents below
like a float of pies
pieces of 'pappadam'
Asia Europe, Africa, Australia
America, the Artic region and the Antarctic
just little islands
on the chest of mighty oceans

looking up from there
there is one colour,
all merged into one reality
universal colour of colourlessness
entire creation levitates
In an air bubble

how insignificant are we
just dust at the feet of the Almighty

Rainbow Falls on the Earth

all through the winter
every plant and animal hibernates
the moment snowflakes flutter
in the sky, the ambience turns
blueish white with shades of grey
greenery frostbitten
resting white Lillies on rooftops
whistling chilly wind
biting weather shrill and sharp

then one day first rays of sunflower
a drizzle of yellow petals
warmth falls in every nook and corner
rhythmic chant of nature
all wake up from deep meditation

with a fine floral garment
she stands there elegantly
decorated with blooms of every colour
spreading intoxicating fragrance
a designer saree wear
adorned with flowers bees and butterflies dancing on soft feet
from petal to petal drunk with
spirits of the spring season
the world turns to rhyme a melody
of singing birds

dreaming world sway and sing
sprinkling colour dust in the air
the celebration begins
rainbow falls on the earth

Stretches Beyond Time

Imagination lies beyond time
into infinity
hands of hope stretched
grabbing the rail
many have travelled this way.
trains filled with passengers
rushed past
giant steam engines earthquake
spitting smoke sneezing steam
engine driver his flannel cap
darkened with smoke and sweat
loud yodelling steam whistle

windows flashed
countless Picasso cubic faces
Van Ghog's sketches
from unknown stations to infinity
immortality on the wings of a raven
innumerable images convoy
through mind

generations change
mammoth pulling machines of
diesel oil, the smell in the air
speeding wheels
long threatening howls

hauling giant bogies,
mile-long goods train

lone passenger the guard
with flag

Dreaming Dawn

on the cheeks of her still hangs
two drops of darkness
far away from the infinity
a sieve is spilling a silvery mist

the daydreamer peeps off
his blond wet hair dripping gold
shades of rainbow swaying
light hum of oceanic waves

dewdrops glide over the glass pane
faded night flowers cover the earth
the stale smell of darkness
night creatures retreat behind the screen

pulling the blanket sleep cuddles
red ants on a cold bite
seeking the warmth of dawn pleasure
listening to the tweaking birds
I wake up to a sweet dreaming dawn

Beedi Shops of Democracy

the barbershop absorbed
clanking of scissors
all the three revolving chairs
occupied by white-covered bodies
artists creating the latest filmy hairstyles.
crew cuts step cuts Amitab style

well dressed hairdressers
busy discussing the latest politics
while smoothing the chins
spraying deodorant

the usual row of readers in the waiting benches
each holding the day's newspaper
periodicals, cinema magazines, star and style
regular visitors visit the saloon
just to read newspapers, magazines
college students for a glance
in the large mirror brush the hair
blaring songs of Kishore Kumar adds more colour

from the next shop a local beedi (country cigarettes)making shop
one worker literate reads the newspaper
for the benefit of listeners who cannot read or write
heating discussions about any subject under the sun
Olympics to Trump's latest eccentrics

the length of Modi's beard
latest Pulitzer Prize winner
death of Danish Siddiqui
from these small beedi shops
Communists came to power in Kerala
through Democratic means

Rainbow Vanishes

frostbitten stars
blue beams standstill
chandelier constellations
crystalline beads
struk bitten by its on light

refraction of rays
Rainbow shades
in the shivering galaxies
the reflection of slated colour glass
streams of pigments
globules of snow

the sun kisses the eyes
dream vanishes
silver ice flakes melt
rainbow disappears

In the Kerb Lives a Hope

beyond horizon
behind magnificent clouds
a herd of wild horses
galloping over the sky
hoofing loudly
stampeding rising coloured dust
golden granules
pigments
stardusts

driving and gliding
the monowheel motor
moves in the bumpy cloud waves
hoping to reach the azure calm sky
under the arch of the rainbow
the septa colours
reflect and refract
in through the prism
of iceblocks

mind gets
multi pigmented
drizzling
"vibgyor"

body gets drenched
in the downpour
like playing Holi
the festival of excitement
spraying hopes of luminosity
in the kerb
lives a hope

Mighty Ocean Takes a Deep Breath

mighty ocean takes a deep breath
soft bubbles of exhalation rise above
she meditates sitting on the reef plateau
Coral lotus visited by winged angels
an assortment of marine flora and fauna

blue satin ribbon seaweeds
dance in ecstasy rising their hoods
a sprinkle of confetti the oceanic bloom
exotic corollas afloat near the reef

angels of the sea mermaids
live in the magnificent palace
adorned with ocean stone necklaces and corals
cobalt sea moves in rhythm

the floor is lit by the angelfishes
a three-ring circus tend with blue roofing
the blare of ocean music
entire marine life on exhibition

At the Tip of a Blade of Grass

yogic sleep
yogi's
stretched body
mind and intellect
floats in the
ocean of tranquillity

slowly a divine mist
consumes
envelops everything, everyone
the mystery
of life
hangs on the timeline
precariously
like a dew
stretching at the tip of
a blade of grass

Dream Merchants

dream merchants were floating
aboard a sailing ship
wind pushing the sail forward
the dream sheds its wing
I wake up to a call of sailors
ahoy ahoy

cobalt blue turf of the sea
we were bumping into the waves
dancing ship in a thrilling voyage
to the fantasy land shaar

the ancient historical map is on display
our ship cruise to the fantasy land beyond the horizon afar the sun and
moon lands

it was a lover's ship taking to a fantasy
onshore of excellence we were dropped
each pair were guided to a magnificent
underground natural caves heavenly abodes sculptured by the magic
of nature

a piped pure music of the ocean and symphony of shaar land of ecstasy
Over the roof the display of glow worms
hibernate into magic wonder

daily we sleep on a bed of rose petals
soft fragrance wakes our pruriency
Everyone strolls wearing birthday suits
the beauty of the fantasy island invoked

Adam and Eve live in the wonderland
the forbidden Apple tree still, grows
spreading elaborate branches with ripe fruits
the hissing hooded snakes dance to the love melody

did we eat the forbidden fruit
I rolled over the bed and fell with a thud
and loud screaming
was it a dream, fantasy or nightmare

Heart-shaped Leaves

the heart-shaped
banyan leaves
braches swing
in the wind
shakes, shivers, vibes
dry leaves fall
a breeze takes them
forming a whirlpool

through the day
she breathes
carbon dioxide
her nostrils exhale
oxygenated
life force

nearby pond
bubbles like DNA chart
water lilies breathe
petals spread
gasping for oxygen

Zombies on the Move

the massive crowd pulling in
a huge procession on the way
slogan shouting fisted hands up in the air holding flags of colours like
smashed
surrealistic live sketching
drumming, firecrackers, faceless men and women supporting the
utopian party

the show of the pre-election
the campaign comes to an end
Very many porcelain characters
assembled on the rostrum
wearing monkey caps in different
colours and shapes, politician little gods of democracy, dummies in
every clownish attire smooth makeover faces.

sharply dyed moustache waxed
groomed cartoon characters, the smile of a Wolf, crocodile weep

like a binalle display, the statues sit erect
promising honey and milk in the public
water taps fortunately no water in the taps, porcelain dolls clatter, and
zombies on the move.

Heritage Hostel

the catcalls, howlings
he stepped in
heritage gate
the boys' hostel
twin sharing room
darkened with smoke
grafitti covered wall
of old students

put your signature
on the Wall
and enter
sound
from infinity
Welcome

Yet We Dream

strings attached mind afloat in the ocean of mortality
yet, we dream, plan the future

 Animated colour pencil
animated colour pencil
jumped danced spoke
in a thin line from the depth
a lovely silky thread stitches
on the medium pinning artist's Imagination

shades transformed
the scenario lime lighted
characters blew up
uni unique colour scheme
the animated subject comes to life
lively expressions

linked animal faces
to human body
comes to life
vivid form

owl-faced blown lady
connected to many faces, and objects around
communicating with the genius
to the viewers to the entire world

awestruck expression
glides from my ink
animated words
face turns owlish

Pathetic Smile

pathetic broad smile
dry parched lips bleeding
yellowish teeth, darkened gums
hunger sleeps in his eyes

the battered shirt fights with time
yet, well dressed
the shoe needs a caring hand to polish
pant slips from his hips

belly retreated
he ate a menu picture
sumptuous meal
after a long time!

Virtual Reality

thoughts wander plucking from the
infinite garden
she wears a unique natural aromatic breeze
adorning a sky-blue muslin gliding over her body
rushing a stallion hoofing kicking the clouds
exposing her subtle silky pink body tones of female sex

her nano digital circuits wake her
transforming into a human-machine
intelligent emotional reactions
her imagination runs wildly strong
induce orgasm and ejaculation

her soft natural smell guides me to
the extremes of virtual reality
then she gets disintegrated.....

Sculptures of Nature

serene solitude, infinite silence
Dawn looms from the meditation
pure silky threads of mist turn into morning
the sculpturer wading through dreams
gold and silver threads interweaved canvas spreading in the horizon

the artist in the depth of Imagination
mixes the pigments in an aesthetic palette
hands swift moves, brush strokes
divine colour blend in unique textures

artisan fills the spaces
lifelike tabletops filled with aromatic steam
sandwiches filled with tasteful fills
colour layers buns, bull's eye,
salt and pepper on the Eastern sky

the table is laid Sun's bull's eye
scrambled egg clouds
fresh orange sun squeezes the juice
he infused his breath in all his paintings
still, the painter signs bold letters
Stillleben mit Zinntellern, Steinkrug und Waffeln (Still life with pewter)

Display

underneath the cobalt ocean
sea flowers swim
calm seabed snores
bubbles of a dream
surface in the brain
the binary signal lights display

Pluto

gods and demigods on a soccer match
well maintained Astroturf
floodlight of constellations
captains sun and Moon referee Jupiter
they made Pluto a football
captain's kick splintered poor Pluto

A Full Woman

suddenly the woman a girl wakes up
the spring season arrives with splendour
exotic flower blooms in every colour
the fragrance of intoxicated earth

donning the designer floral saree
she arrives and strolls softly with her shoe flower feet
as she smiles pearls litter around
her half-opened dreamy intoxicated eyes

pink face where dimples smile
dark blue eyes peacock quill eyelashes
Shiny sensitive roseate lips
well-dressed ponytail hairstyle

thousands of silky butterflies clothed her body
an assortment of pigmented wings swing
move in rhythmic dancing waves
her body exposed as they lifted the angelic wings often

as time passes she becomes a lover
a wife, a mother
she faces the world with courage, confidence
only she can give birth to a baby
and a father too
yes she had a metamorphosis
to a full matured confident woman

Devil's Dinner

Frankenstein's favourite snack was
frankenberries sandwiches
with toppings of wimpy marbles

he had his jaws reconstructed for his daily refreshments
also, he relished snapshooter tooter wraps
on the rock stirred not shaken

woofenspittle toot and scoot was his
famous past time invented himself
a card game mystery or mastery
always he won
once he explained his winning streaks
whenever a maggot sits on the card of any player he wins
Mr Frankenstein used to be the one and only winner
as he applies honey stealthily on his card

he keeps a souvenir of a tooth collection
of his opponents' ty beetsie blow holes in their tooth chains.

he lives in his Palacious mansion
Cramp slips the knot with his wife Mrs Frankenstein
she cooks for him a devil's dinner daily

Salabanjika Waiting for Her Lover

she was a particle of a cosmic dream
an Angel of perfection pulchritude
jumped through galaxies, kissed constellations
swam in the flow of Milkyway

made costumes of silky mist
decorated with star sequence
blue ribbon clouds, cosmetics from snow white
wore her star-studded crown
necklace of blue stars
stardust paste on her dark hair

when the sun comes down she wears him
on her forehead as vermilion
his pink her roosh blush
awaits her lover moon with a rainbow-beaded garland

Fantasy Land

nature is blended here
hands of creation embrace
the whole of Magic Land
which is afloat in the south china sea

the statue of the deity lord Muruga
overlooks Malaysia with a blessing palm
very picturesque Coastal plains
interior, jungle-covered mountains interlocked with the land mass

a cable ride to the Genting Heights
world's largest hotel welcomes you
with beautiful colour schemes
exotic food delicacy pulls off tiredness

a visit to Petronas Twin Towers,
Islamic Arts Museum, Langkawi Cable Car, Langkawi Sky Bridge,
Menara KL Tower,
lifts one to the heights of fantasy
botanical garden entwined
with vines of our imagination

exotic rare orchids bloom
fine-dressed birds from all around the world
experts interact with them with a theme
chocolate factory with sweet delicacies

among the chimes of prayer bells
divine calls from mosques
announcing prayer time
sweet singing from the church choir

sleepwalking
to kl international Airport
wakes you up from a fantasy land

To the Land of Mystery

for a few moments
she was gliding through
a fantasy
her face touching the petal feather pillows
eyes filled with desires
Cupid's arrow
she visioned her lover

her silky soft skin
covered with velvet bedsheet
touch of her body
awakened extrinsic nature
rainbow feature
angel butterflies bloomed
her alluring body

ultimately
she got wings
a fairy Queen flew away
to the land of mystery
aesthetic Hobbiton

Magician of the Universe

scintillating flute music
channelling through the valley
Crystal water flows through Yamuna
grazing cows their dark wide eyes
bathing gopikas
the intoxicating smell of sandal paste.

silent serenity
imagery of pareekshith
little Krishna
his unique azure divine colour
little crown small earrings
elegant waist chain
anklets diamond bangles
kousthuba

the swish of yellow silk
a moving flute
nodding peacock quills
a cascade of blueish dark clouds

two feet moving
soft silent footfall
the imprint of lotus feet
smiling blooms
fragrance of basil

yes he is near
pure butter balls move in the air
yes he is born
in every heart
magician of the universe

Yes Last Days of Summer

the dawn arrived shaking quills on treetops
wet dry spots of a drizzle on the courtyard
pieces of littered rainbow among dark clouds
squirrels are busy salvaging the last dry mango nut for the monsoon
pied cuckoo spotted with thrilling songs
the smell of earth after the first rain fills the air

Elevated High Plane

elevated high plane
dwarfed the giants
in enlightenment world
rolls in the palm
universe a gooseberry
trains and planes
centipede and mosquito

The Giant Feet of the Ocean

the giant feet of the ocean
slowly strolls onto the bed
a mountainous great wall
formed with turquoise waves

mixing pigments of nature
the underworld turned into a wild exhibit of marine creatures
grandpa turtle takes a daily dip in the sea
shining his designer heritage shell

like a lighthouse of knowledge
he preserves protects marine life

A Seraphic Moment

that was a seraphic moment
the urine droplet spread
the indicator on the strip
shy happiness-filled fear

wrapped up day
of unknown happiness
with a candlelight dinner
body changes
becoming a woman

topographic strips
delightful dye contours
womb of mother earth
filled with lovely pigments
anxiously
smiling motherhood lactate.

Nobody Knows

nobody knows
they have a Newfoundland
there they hangout

sitting on a row
under the feet a humming electric wire
feet clutched tight
and they talk turning sideways
want you wanna do?

a raven caw
one flap out his wings
just flutter away with speed
the silencer free bike
makes fumes,
supersonic accilator noice

all follow in a gang
in black Blazers
girls and boys rushing in and out
thousands of drones
waiting for the Queen

they are on a trampoline
hiking up and down
twisting turning twirling
by the time a metamorphosis

waiting for the metro
holding executive briefcases
bespectacled MBAs
there are new gen monkies
squatting for another show

Denim

their sun woke up in the village
from the blue ocean
splashing ultramarine waves
ryots had their dhotis
spotted with cerulean

British planters found
it is cheaper to exploit Indian farmers
forced cultivation of indigo
wages were low, cheap labour
slave masters had their eyes
fixed on cobalt blue profits

then ryots were in a riot
they refused to cultivate indigo
for British slave masters
and factories were closed

the denim you wear
has a revolutionary theme
ultramarine blue eyes
blue-blooded royal greed
the mountain of light
still adorn the crown of England

Monsoon Symphony

the rhythmic trickle of rain strings
celestial jaltharangamm percussion
melody tone as it falls into lakes
clouds drumming frantic monsoon thunderstorms

veins of lightning
touches the rainbow
flashing fiddling cello tones
Producing seven notes
sa ree ga ma pa tha nee
western notes
DO, RE, MI, FA, SOL, LA, and TI.
the rainbow melts and streams down
in seven tones septa pigments
the whole earth's horripilate sings
seventh symphony of Beethoven
drops of songs dance on the tips of leaves on every blade of grass
nightingales sing melodiously

mother earth's music
a lullaby for every being and non-beings for a meditative deep sleep
listen to tones of sitar strings cascade through roof tiles in a row striking
cords of the mind

Memories

you are frozen
in my self
like an idol
worshipped
daily
lighting a wick
offered
an incense
you were
the sweet aromatic
memory

My Creation

the cool mystic fog
wonder of aurora
striking complexion change
laser beams
in elegant hues
filling the cloud patterns
gliding rainbow

behind the backdrop
In the canvas
my brush strokes deciphered
a young vibrant damsel

my brush dedicated
delicately touched my belle
I carved her out of my depth
breathed life
she had a velvet skin
angelic countenance
smell of lotus
lips of rose petals

one last stroke
she slowly strolled in
her pink feet
glided into my desires
my creation

Glow-worm

through the pitch-dark space
I trekked the black hole
accidentally my hands touched
a glow worm
saw a thousand suns
hiding in her blossom

Emerald

Time Stands Still

Time stands still.
In the cobweb,
teardrops still
hangs.
entangled life
tries a feeble breathe.
Forest fire licks
everything away.
A sermon half delivered
echoes.
we hope for his
resurrection.

Sleeping Dream

I just saw
a piece of moon
on the tree top.
It was
my dream
sleeping
silently.
I await
till she wakes up
to reality.

I Remain

There is an incredible indescribable feeling.
A comfort so subtly enveloped in your presence.
My words and intellect cannot conceive,
your benevolent magnanimous nature.

Though you are near far yet not clear,
your next step still keeping the suspense.
your silent actions speak volumes.
Oh, Mother of all how and what shall I call you?

How can I contain you in a name and form?
Attributes are insufficient to tag you on.
Oh Mother Nature you are beyond words
Are you, not the one who created this world?

You are the one who vacuums it out.
My imaginations fall short to adorn you.
Between the magic of time, matter and space.
You create beauty everywhere in perfection.
Then vanish deep into the sound of silence.
My images fall short failing to contain you.
As I fumble in the darkness of my ignorance,
You spark a thought of your effulgence
Shedding the weight of my identity I merge into you
We delve into timeless intoxication!

A Mural of Reality

She put on makeup.
looking elegant and mode
walked into a magic mirrors room.
All types of her images danced there.
Tall, short, fat, vulgar, fearful,
awful reflections of same face.
life is like that of many masks.
Picasso painted a montage of life.
A mural of reality.

Hot Chase

On a hot chase,
heated with emotions
we merge,
into one soul.
we melt down
to ecstasy,
and become,
one flow of life.
Nothing exists,
But one.

As My Dream

He covers my body
with soft petal kisses
 each cell
 dances ecstasy
blankets of butterflies
colourful wings
flap with a hiss

I moved
my body shivered
they flew away
in a flutter of designer wings
a nude surprise
as my smile lit the azure sky
as my dream.

Heartbeats

Miles to go.
The mind stretches beyond.
thoughts silhouette,
Cast many shades.
A stream of images
Trickle-down.
where am I?
I feel deserted.
I lost my path.
Was on,
Trail of a foot print.
That too ends here.
lost in the desert.
I hear howling,
Murmurs.
Memories of the past,
Hanging upside down,
As bats.
Fly around.
Their red eyes haunt,
A drizzle,
Drenched me.
A strong beam of light,
Lit my frame.
I wake up to reality.
There is a blaring,
Drumbeat.
My heart beats.

God sent him to teach love and create life.

Legacy

Here is the valley of splendour,
where once Aphordite lived.
She brought a piece of heaven to earth
and created a kingdom of beauty.
When she smiled there was sunlight.
She opened her eyes wide to spill moon light.
Moon, sun and stars danced here,
to the tunes of singing rivulets.
The cosmic rhythm was swinging across.
there was a twinkle of stardust
adorning the meadow, grooves and streams.
When she talked pearls spilt around.
Life was calm and quiet and peaceful.
Sands quivered with pleasure at her footfall.
She erected a rainbow down the river,
lit the streets with diamonds of her love.
Then one day she fell in love with time,
they eloped into infinity,
leaving the valley into the hands of nature,
lonely dale waits for her.
let us protect her legacy.

From the tsunami of time
She came in riding an elephant.
She had hidden the world
Under her scarlet gown.
The elegance of creation wings
into infinity, in search of effulgence.
The tide of her emotions reflects.
She looks into the world awestruck.

We Fell in Love

Her skin was marked
With tattoos of seasons
I painted the sun on her chest
A thousand sunrises
Scorching over my body.
We fell in love.

Life and Death

Between thin wall
of life and death,
behind a misty veil
of ignorance,
awaits a hand raised
in desperation,
gasping
yearning to be rescued
from the filth
of past sins.

Virgin Forest

In the wilderness of forest,
manifestation of beauty
in its subtle cute sweetest forms.
Nature lies stretched intoxicated in love.
Under the canopy of trees,
waits for an angel in her best.
Serenity drizzles all around.
Suspense hides in curves and bends
The long treaded path awaits,
to hear the footfall of her time.
Ears are wide open,
listening for any sounds of life.
When this long wait will end?
Diana sits there in elegance,
eyes planted to infinity.
still anxious to hear the galloping
of her prince's horse.
Virgin forest conceives fears of a tormentor.

Silence of Night

A sensual warm kiss of dawn
opens up a honey pod.
Hot pursuit
on pink velvety petals
smear dew drops.
Passion plough deep
Beetles love
meditating
inside" petal-reefs",
Love and lust
remains ageless.
Orgasmic flow continues,
knocking silence of the night.

A Pearl

As life treks in long strides, the traveller pauses and sits back to relax.

Eyes take a lion's review, he roars louder splitting all boundaries.

Life had covered a long distance, to a destination unknown.

Many tracks lead to infinity strewn with footprints that have passed through the milestones of history created by erecting monuments of time.

Slowly civilization turned around, heels paved the way for wheels.

I x-rayed my mind with a remote thought and found a little bit of creativity ticking.

I imagined a rock rolling down It was to become my wheel of today.

Poured some water to drink in a plastic glass.

An apple that fell on my head again reminded me of a story of a great scientist.

Then one day I heard eureka, eureka from the air, Someone ran across streaking in my mind.

In a subtle mood, I retreated to solitude as time paraded before my closed eyes unaware.

My pensive mood dived deeper and deeper as I meditated in the hands of awareness lost myself in the abyss of brilliance and got dissolved in the light of my images.

I became part of this universe, I ran shouting "Aham Brahmasmi"my sound was echoing from all beings and non-beings." I am the truth" I discovered my identity! by serendipity, A Pearl

Author notes

Syllable Counter Results

Number of Syllables: 324

Words with syllables counted programmatically: serendipitya (5), truthi (2), brahmasmimy (5), aham (2), retreated (3), streaking (2), airsomeone (3), rayed (0), erecting (3),

Tornado

Holding hands of love

we got dissolved in our dreams

crushed by lusty winds

Author notes

Number of Syllables: 17

Words with syllables counted programmatically: N/A

Words: 14

Characters

(all | no spaces | with spaces): 83 | 62 | 77 (Sequential spaces are not counted)

Lines: 3 (Including empty lines)

Letters (number of each): There are 2's. There are 1 b's. There are 1 c's. There are 7 ds. There are 5 e's. There are 1 f's. There are 2 g's. There are 3 hs. There are 4 i's. There are 4 l's. There are 1 m's. There are 4 n's. There are 6 o's. There are 3 rs. There are 7 s's. There are 2 t's. There are 3 u's. There are 2 v's. There are 2 w's. There are 2 y's.

Delight

the beauty of life
is created with a brush
dipped in my delight

Author notes
Number of Syllables: 17
Words with syllables counted programmatically: N/A
Words: 13
Characters
(all | no spaces | with spaces): 74 | 51 | 65 (Sequential spaces are not counted)
Lines: 3 (Including empty lines)
Letters (number of each): There are 3 a's. There are 2 b's. There are 1 c's. There are 4 ds. There are 7 e's. There are 2 fs. There are 1 g's. There are 4 hs. There are 6 i's. There are 2 l's. There are 1 m's. There are 1 n's. There are 1 o's. There are 2 p's. There are 2 rs. There are 2 s's. There are 5 t's. There are 2 u's. There are 1 w's. There are 2 y's.
Syllable counter dictionary, syllable rules, haiku syllable counter, syllable counter algorithm, syllable counter and divider, and syllable counter and separator.

We Need

if we did, let us exhume

we need love to live

Author notes

Number of Syllables: 17

Words with syllables counted programmatically: N/A

Words: 15

Characters

(all | no spaces | with spaces): 93 | 49 | 65 (Sequential spaces are not counted)

Lines: 3 (Including empty lines)

Letters (number of each): There are 1 b's. There are 5 ds. There are 11s. There are 1 f's. There are 1 h's. There are 4 i's. There are 4 l's. There are 1 m's. There are 1 n's. There are 3 o's. There are 1 r's. There are 1 s's. There are 2 t's. There are 3 u's. There are 3 v's. There are 3 w's. There are 1 x's. There are 1

Trapped in Time

Somewhere in time, we met
We marked a date in our heart
We admired each other every day
talked silly words, acted strangely
Scratched each other's back
We dreamed together
Weaved silky thoughts around
Created air castles
Teased each other, made fun
We smelled our bodies with love
Exchanged passionate kisses
Twisted our tongues
We pleaded, proposed, and married
Took a solemn oath, saying I. do I do
Monotony consumed us with a yawn
One day we fought for nothing
Tattooed our hearts with teeth and nails
Inflicted wounds of eternal ego
Departed showing our backs to each other
Do you hear a confused feeble cry of a child,
Trapped in time?

Desolation

My dear swan convey him
This loneliness is eating me away
Just have a look in my eyes
Invoke my reflection in your retina
Pass on my images as you see
Describe to him what do see in me
My longing eyes waiting for him
My cheeks and chin miss his kisses
My lips quiver for his lips
My body cannot wait for his fondle
Oh my dear swan listen to my heartbeat
It sings a melody of love
A sonnet of my soul
Convey my heart's song in his ears
I cannot wait any more! this desolation

Compulsive Eater

When time breaks out and shatters
our dreams are broken,
we step over the carcasses of our dreams.
life freezes below minus point celsius
we become fossils in between time and space
dead memories sleep under mountainous history
once excavated our broken clocks turn into exhibits
we the dead species displayed in the museums
all will be wrapped in the sheets forgotten memories
mummified under the clothes of mystery
Time is a compulsive eater and unsatisfied customer.

In Chirping Tones

she was a friend of birds
every day she cooked food for them
took it to a secret place
where she met and fed them all
she talked in bird language
communicated effectively
each of her friends had a name she gave
they responded to her call
she nursed mother birds
when they had their chicks
looked after them like a mother
she often became their rest place
by standing still for them to relax
she was the mother of all
and still, she wears a feather cap
that was bestowed on her
by the mother nature
often she sings a song for birds
in chirping tones

Smile You Are in a Candid Camera

I know you are a sweet cute girl
with full of power and dare
you only have to lift the blinds
see the beam of light stretch in
there is a beautiful world outside
with full of thrust and energy
a brave new world kicking
there is a touch of God in everything
he beckons you to feel him
he touches you with his hands of breeze
he sings for you through birds
he smiles at you with flowers
can't you smell his fragrance around
just sit under the sun you will feel his warmth
he showers a rain of love on you
Oh the trees invite you to rest under
do not miss the first blue snowflakes
he may turn out any moment riding a sledge
with your presents your Santa
please listens to the chime of time
watch the birds fly like fairies
just listen to the music of life, dear
watch the night azure sky glitter
don't you want to see a celestial canopy
decorated with stars and moon
and angels float on their ecstatic wings?

Just open your doors and windows
open your wide dreamy beautiful eyes
let the elegance of the world peep in
smile, you have nothing to lose
but your four walls of confusion
oh the entire galaxy is waiting for you
smile you are in a candid camera

Poem of My Soul

On a high realm
she floats on a lotus
of wisdom,
the muse of
all aesthetics.
in the subtle
the serenity of my mind
I invoked her.
To my surprise,
I found the
the wonder of the universe,
all creations
gliding through
her bosom.
I squat at her feet,
awestruck, unable to pen
a word to delineate
her elegance.
I drop my tears
as a verse
from my soul.

Timeless Time

The clock is broken down.
there are steps leading
to timelessness.
just plunge into the ocean
lose time sense
and be timeless time.

Her Soul

all you have to do
is break the chain
of darkness
let luminous emerge
and sparkle the soul
of night.

Old Man Child

Falling into the labyrinth of time
life gets entangled in the wrinkles
of pains and suffering
until such time we concealed
ourselves with means and devises
grey hair painted to a dark
until it refuses to accept
any shading.
one day you stopped colouring
abandoned makeover kits
an old man comes out of a veil
fully exposed
shivering and shaking
skin loosened
wearing an innocent toothless smile
you are an old man child
without any mask!

A Tribute to My Mother*

Those days will never come back.
The day, I was born into your hands.
I still see your soft smile of happiness,
trying to drip down your cheeks.

You tickled my senses exposed.
I am nourished by your breasts.
you watched me with anxiety care
I slept in the warmth of your love.
Often pinched your hands for comfort

My dreams woke up with your lullaby.
You guided me at each step.
Spent sleepless nights when I fell sick,
wiped my urine and excretion.

I don't know mother how to repay you.
I never wished to see you die.
But silently one day you left.
Never bothered to call me.

While posing for the last snap that I took,
You had the same smile when you saw me first
Your first baby boy!
had the same wonder when I called you my mother.

Oh, my sweet mother, I have never been a good son.
I never have repaid anything!
You were always, always a good mom.
But mother I loved you always.
I still can smell your hair oil in my heart.
Bless me, mother, bless me, mother.

* She left for her heavenly abode on 30 July 2012

Many Scenes

Scene 1
The glow of your face
reflected in my heart
I presented you with a bouquet
reflecting the colour of my heart.
On the east and west in dawn and dusk
every day you lit a wick,
placed a vermilion dot,
on the forehead of the horizon.
You bathed in the sea of tranquillity,
smearing your glazing hue
on the shore of peace.
I used to watch your salinity.

Scene 2
Bamiyan images of Buddha
just got erased
The fierce fire melted rock sculptures
There goes the peace
the peace he preached.

Scene 3
World trade centre
The edifice, pride of civilization,
culture and democracy
got a blowup page

in the annals of human cruelty.
Watch the memorial monument,
You can see tears still streaming down,
into infinity.

Scene 4

The metals of a train bogie got red
Mumbai still weeps silently.
The charred remains of
Innocent breadwinners
Lie scattered in the barren minds
the railroad and Taj Mahal
looked at the world
with expectation.

Scene 6

When a nation involves
In creating a towering inferno
It is the worst of all crimes.
Our silent cries were heard by blind ears.
The perpetrators lavish
in the excreta of their crime.
The maggots on human flesh
fly around.

Scene 7

Cowards aimed and maimed
the innocent liberal crowds of Paris.
Bombs flowered six times
smashing the lives of innocents.
How dare you create a Guernica,
with flesh and blood

of humanity.
Shame on you shame on you.
After all, what did you gain?
Oh my dear Paris
wake up do not cry
let me wipe your tears
here take my handkerchief
wipe wipe wipe your sorrow
lie on the lap of the mother world.

Let the drama end here forever
Come to the serenity of love
Equilibrium of peace
Live and let live

Living in a Deluge

In the depth of my fantasy
I fondled my white cats.
I had drowned in the abyss of love,
listening to the mew of my pets.
I smiled.
my emotions streamed.
was sucked into a whirlpool
I was in a strange world
living in a deluge.
I sat on the coral reef
with contentment,
imagining
a world full of my children roaming
my little fur-clad hopes,
and their burrrrr echoing,
in my heart,
in my soul,
I sit here in ecstasy.

Reality Stares

Squeezed through the time
age wrinkles
body contracts
in best-dressed Sundays
body rattles in the suit
youth had retreated
back into your mind
the face expresses a hollow
yellow teeth make the smile
more horrible
unaware life strolls
on bracketed old legs
words, mouth, tongue,
and tastes recede
on a stroke-struck face
reality stares at you
with a howl.

Ecstatic Silence

in the valley divine
glaze and glitter flowers
from the roots of love
grace of creation
enchants
the aroma of elegance spreads
filling the breeze
with freshness
dew lives on the tips of
silky leaves
reflecting the hue
of the world
in its excellence
eyes wide lips half open
awestruck
I remain in rhapsodic
silence.

Take Three for the Price of One!

Shopping malls are opened
on every nook and corner.
people flock in masses
attracted into the trap lights
insects get in with a buzz!
on the shelves colourful display
of stuff in all brands
waiting with a hook and line
the bait is tempting you.
you pick all the odd things
put in the trolley
push ahead with a heap of trappings.
at the counter you pay
using your plastic money
getting a discount of five per cent
on every purchase worth a fortune!
the poor customer walks out
with the pride of earning a discount
several junk goods in possession.
take one, get two at the price of one.
the poor chap went to buy a safety pin
ended up shopping at a mall
the current of Oniomania
would strike any moment anywhere
beware they have nothing to lose
but you have, your credit card
defaulted payment!
credibility

Lace of Elegance

intricately knitted black lace
cover the moons
milky white drizzles
grace flow incessantly
the body emits a golden aura
beauty cascades over her body
her beautiful hair tickles the breeze

a spider is at work
weaves a designer web
around her
a world is created
form her womb
she smiles
a mother is born
under the lace of elegance

A Drop in the Ocean of Time

I have no idea where I come from

I looked back to my life it is a total blank

I see a long trekked path with footprints on it...

I looked down to earth, it was tickling my feet

over my head, I see a flowing blue current

it was studded with diamonds and golden pendants

I am still confused to know that I don't know

then I view deep into the future, that too is vague

I see a long paved path of mystery with fuzzy logic

then I answered myself, you are a drop in the ocean of time

One Kiss

One kiss I can melt you down or suck you in, Your choice!

Imagination

I was diving in the depth of the deep sea
moving along with a colourful heard
I flapped my fins with excitement
was living, moment by moment in a stimuli
my emotions flooded along with
the aromatic percolation of the beauties around
they took me on their wings and carried me away
into the wonderland of disguise
suddenly turning into a cuttlefish
I copulated with umpteen beauty of nature
my eyes were wide open enjoying pulchritude
jumping back to reality I raised my crimson face

The next day I was on the beach surrounded by bikinis
imagining myself a cuttlefish

Now I Am Free

Now I am free
to meet the wilderness
with the spirit of a horse.
ride me until dawn
I gasp
saliva dripping
let me see if I can
sustain
roughness
of terrain.
embrace
real freedom
and runaway
like a hurricane.
hair on my nape flows
against wind.
my ponytail
swing and dances
declaring my liberty.

Window Display

designer skirt
with model
for sale

Lips of Fire

heart-shaped sponge cake is ready
tastefully decorated
topped in colourful icing sugar
wrapped in a thin film of edible sprinkles
seasoned with nuts and dry fruits
the cake is filled with juicy tones
honeydew granules
anyone tastes it will be on a trip to ecstasy
the potion of love
rest on the lips of fire

Unfolding

Let me capture you with a net of emotions,
then I foment you with my warmth,
netted you as my exotic butterfly.
with the wings of my lofty imagination
I coloured your wings with soft hues.
made elaborate tattoos on my dreams.
You tickled my body and soul
As tender as a feathery breeze.
I carried you as a paragon of reverie.
Opening your wings of purity,
you flew me away into pleasant hallucinations.
Slowly I found myself flying with celestial wings.
We made our day by unfolding our fantasies.

Shadow

I was sitting face to face with the lord
he had duplicated me off his shade
was in thoughts looking at me closer
but made me feel by placing the five senses

with a touch of his palm, he put his heart in
I was in full glow wading into the womb of time
became a tinny little embryo of his vision
taking shape into a divine form of life

I was born into the hands of invisible
was in hibernation behind the time
he had me charged with my past actions
then filled me with egoistic desires and delusions

time pushed me to the world of unknown
a pair of eyes watched me, cared for me,
fed me with the nectar of love from breasts
my mother enthralled me and filled me.

my odyssey began again in the life
many seasons arrived and gone before me
leaving a tattoo on my person every time
a shadow was following me all the time

I trekked a long way into unknown terrain
nausea and fatigue joined me on the way
my skin had faded, and loosened, bones rattled
I had to end my sojourn abruptly, consuming my shadow

Am I a Poet?

I strongly believe I am not a poet.
Never assimilated any classic poems,
Not studied any classics or modern poems.
But I read novels and other English writings as a passion.
Poetry came to me as a shy girl,
dressed in sweet shades and glow.
She winked at me, seduced me,
unaware I fell in love with her.
Holding hands we trekked many terrains,
visited wonderlands and monuments on earth.
I carried you in my hands as a dream.
We searched our souls with wild hugs.
I crushed you to the chest of my emotions.
You flowed into me as streams of love.
erected your multi-faceted images,
consecrated you with a shower of purity.
I unstripped your enigmatic clothing.
You baffled me with nudity of emotions.
Unaware dawn and dusk entwined.
we rode on a swing shaking the world up n 'down.
My sweet muse! yet you remain a puzzle.
My words cannot clothe you and uncover you.
I am a tiny little concoctor of words.
You are an ocean with enchanting waves.
I am an urchin standing, basking on the shore.
Awestruck, visualizing unfathomable
depths of your mighty whirlpool.

Intolerance Boils Down

I have no share in this blood.
the time of the day
seeps through the hands.
killings, slaughter,
murder, order of the day

every second
someone dips his hand
in the blood of innocent,
places the bloody palm
on the walls of humanity.
we are piranhas
nibbling lives to bare bones.
a world of chaos is taking shape.
intolerance boils down to,
dripping down all over
disfiguring mankind...

You Blinded Us

Mother started living
when you entered her womb
glowing her hopes.
one day you drained
aborting her motherhood.
baby, you left us
hollowing our beliefs
now living in our memories.

Myths

She left behind a colourful world
transcended desires,
attained her tranquillity,
delved deep into the mystery of life.
all the pain and sorrow of the world haunted her,
it flowed off her body and eyes as black tears!
she killed her mind.
compassion flowed out.
she created a lot of myth images,
milked them with love and grace.
she became a mirror of the world
reflecting every scene of life.
the sun shines far behind clouds.
night pulls a drape, the azure sky shines,
with stars in the milky way of galaxies,
moon flows down in streams of passion.
there is scope for a brilliant show on earth

Humanoid

Living in the darkness of time
body and mind get harder
we develop feelers of steel
nerves of steel strings
our eyes glow like cat's eyes
a humanoid is born unaware
under the limelight of divinity
man realizes his weakness
he bows down before the might
stoops at the knees of almighty

Like a Raven

I saw you sleeping
your eyes are half closed
mouth open
saliva was dripping
from the corner of your lips
your were snoring
a rub on the rock
with a coconut shell
your clothes untidy
exposing your midriff

a sharp alarm got you up
yawning
you raised your hands up
went away
like a raven

Destiny

In the troubled waters of life,
I am rowing a boat of time.
the boat sways and swings,
as turbulence continues.
the sea was roaring with high waves.
the little lantern also blew off.
my rudderless boat spins and turns
my hope still rests ahead.
somewhere in the sky
a flint of a thunderbolt
I lie flat in the watercraft
praying the lodestar
to guide me wherever
it leads to a destiny unknown.

Service to Life

He was sleeping on a silky bed of love and care.
dim-lit room was watched by maids for sure.
he dreamed a dream brocaded in glitter and colour.
with happiness braided with a rainbow of his life so rare.
king made sure he was inside the palace walls.
never wanted him to see the miseries of the world.
teachers of all faculties taught him indoors.
he lived without knowing anything about life outer
one day prince forced his teacher to take him for a walk.

he enjoyed the beauty, freshness and fairness of nature.
while on the road, he saw men and women in a loincloth
beggars stretching hands for alms, sick and wounded in agony
the boy wondered about, strange scenes all around.

he never had witnessed such a pathetic scenario before.
suddenly he heard women crying and men carrying a body.
his teacher explained to him about death and dying.
he realized all have to die one day or the other.

that night he could not eat or sleep on the lap dream.
he tossed on the bed realizing his aim of birth.
suddenly he got up and slipped off the palace.
he was in search of happiness for all beings.

he travelled the length and breadth of the kingdom.
experienced agony of life, desolation, despair n' trauma.
all he could experience during the long trek of his life.
meditating under the cool shades of a BodhI tree of grace

he realized the reason for men's sorrow and mortality.
preached his finding by travelling every nook and corner.
practised non-violence taught the nobility of sacrifice
The truth of the cause of suffering (samudaya)
The truth of the end of suffering (nirhodha)
The truth of suffering (dukkha)
The truth of the path that frees us from suffering (magga)

"I slept and dreamt that life was a joy. I awoke and saw that life was service. I acted and behold, service was a joy."
Rabindranath Tagore

Author notes
I am not sure if this poem suits the subject. But I have done my best Not very rhyming.

Coral Reef

He gave a tight long kiss
vermilion on her forehead spread
she took a dip in the sea
her wet long hair was dripping pearls
golden globules splashed in the sea
while the sun was showering saffron petals on her
her nudity was covered with soft corollas
her smile glowed in the evening sun
the radiant lady walked away
sprinkling a live sonnet
she was possessed
walked in unsteady steps
her hair was cascading like a coral reef

5/7/5 [I said hi to Ku]
 I said hi to Ku
she said to hype syllables
I bowled over her

Entwined Fond Memories

Intimacy is silence
silence is louder
a look
smile
soft caress
by unique sound
creates adoration
you just bloom
aroma spread.
only she or he can sense
squeeze drip
of sweet ambrosia of love
your soul.
those who
sense it
will drink
along with you
like an entwined
fond memories

Hourglass

Many visited this earth.
many departed.
many live here.
Everyone lives,
holding an hourglass.
sand grains depart
merge with past time
when the top tier emptied
you are done.
we hold in our palms,
a heap of dust,
a hand full of dust
full of history.
each grain had been a part,
actively watched the wheel
roll through seconds.
war and peace.
riot of ryots
great men at war.
dictators,
isms,
all left without a trace.
but great men,
saints they lived,
leaving their footprints,
on earth.

a trail for us to follow,
reach.
the ultimate
destiny of life.

Let It Not Happen

Well, it is our secret desire,
to start world war three!
why because the human mind,
craves for a black sun!
pain, loots and sadistic pleasures
are enjoyed by megalomaniacs.
who will be the next Hitler?
is the million-dollar question.
next war will be a cyber encounter
a cyber-maniac will own this earth
he will have a multi-mega supercomputer.
running in a space station
controlling universal economic activities
by the click of a mouse
all the wealth and weaponry of nations shall be
syphoned off to a villainy vault
resulting in a new world order! Turmoil?

The Beauty of Silence

Transcend ten words
what remains is muteness
beauty of silence

I Found Her Holding Me Again

The train started with a jolt
slowly the station drifted away
a collage of faces just faded
remains in the retina
I was trying to create a montage
passengers settle in their pursuit
I tried to figure out the lone face
the eyes were anxious
there was a drip of sorrow on the face
a searching look fell on me
suddenly she was running behind
I leapt with my anxiety
later I dived of the window
I found her holding me again

Bitter-gourd

I have no idea where to dig for my soul.
I skimmed through the ocean of life for it
I did not get butter and I got bitter gourd!
I am eating my bitterness with sugary dreams,

Wake Up

Tears of tomorrow
started from yesterday
it is concealed
forming a lake

a desert is advancing
eating away
all on the way
dunes
move swiftly across
water is hiding
behind mirage
we live in delusion
a heat wave strike
we get burned
yet we feel
comfort in the
air conditioner
our Oasis

we are sure
the lake of tears will burst
let it explode
who cares
we live in a dream castle
in deep slumber

My Heritage Home

My heritage home stands aloof.
It has the looks of a deserted grandma.
Grand old maple trees cast a shadow on her,
as if giants trying to grab a scared goat.
Courtyard was littered with dry maple leaves,
scratches my heart, disturbing my mind.
Scratch wounds bleed paining my soul.
Long corridor silhouetted by giant pillars.
Grand old mahogany trees overlook the home.
Moon swings on swaying shades of its trunk,
fades away slowly behind dark clouds.
Rooms in the house witnessed many events.
Birth, death, weddings, joy and happiness,
success and failures, dreams and reality.
Religious festivities are celebrated in pomp.
Every cry n sigh of the family stays in,
echoes on four walls of my maternal home.
sweat and tears vaporized; hangs.
Dark oil stains remain on pillows, as shades of the past.
Still, I could sleep in here with peace,
as if leaning on the lap of grandma,
holding on to her soft long ear loops,
she grew over time.
The last one who departed was grandma.
I feel her fondle her dry fingers.
I see her muscles shiver in her loose skin.

But, still, I can see her half smile.
Comforting, cooling my boiling mind.
dreaming a whole lot of nostalgia,
I dive slowly into folds of sleep.

Divine Thoughts

flooding with thoughts
mind asphyxiated by nausea
it is like a garbage can overflowing
stinks and spreads poison
wonder if a man can have
a child's mind pure and pellucid
purity brings freedom
freedom is liberation
just calm the mind
fill it with divine thoughts
peace and prosperity befall

Liberator

The day I was born he was born behind.
somebody follows me unaware all through my life.
it is there irritating, sometimes he is at the front,
he trails me, I run, and he runs too.
I squat, and he does so.
where ever he is there.
when I sleep he awaits.
he is the shadow of my life.
he may strike any time where,
he is the liberator who pushes me out of time.

Tributary

Unaware nature sleepwalked into a stream,
where beauty takes a shower in the rivulet.
covering her body with a negligee of mist
she was screaming her grace to the valley.
Her thoughts flow as exquisiteness of bliss.
Her golden gown rests behind her on shore.
Intoxicated she holds a magic wand of elegance.
becoming a tributary of consciousness into hearts

River of Love {The Mountains and Waterfalls}

Beauty cascade
from quality
subtle thoughts drizzle
on mountains
follows a trail
flows into,
jump to
wilderness
embraces purity of nature
the hearts of mound
pours down
as streams of
romance, consciousness
ultimately
reaches a sea of tranquillity
river is connected
to the summit
hugging, winding
with hands of
love.
Roots of antiquity
 Rooted in mystery
spirits of time howl
beneath the roots of history

many lie covered in dust
they are forgotten
faded into oblivion
they came and lived here
signed the visitor's book
making their life an example
when they were on earth
they moved and lived
in every heart
made a moment of their own
fought for righteousness
they departed without any claims
we discounted them
for a few silver coins
when loneliness creeps
we pray in their memory
light a candle on their tombs
we live proudly in their antiquity

Respect Them

Women are not mere
woe women
beneath fragility
it is time to grow
nerves of steel
and fist of iron

but let life bloom
bear fruits
spread fragrance
of love

God created
universe
from the womb
of women
respect them

Happy Melodies

Happiness states a state of mind
we live in a dream playing with many toys
discard them often
craving continues
new gadgets arrive
gets obsolete
you don't stop
one day you find a beggar sleeping in you
kicked him off his filthy greed
you found humming happy melodies now

D Dreamy Words

Delve into the depth to find pearls of words
Dream up a verse filled with honey loads

Louder Than Loudest

A sound, decipher it into syllables
then thoughts follow words
mix emotions, it flows through
love, anger, compassion
cascade all expressions.
some times it is fire, creating an inferno
a world war.
wise ones remain silent.
muteness speaks louder than loudest

Wanderings

I was wandering in the wilderness of virginity
modesty retained my explorative freedom
I was covered in a rob of feminine shyness
but you uncovered me with the tip of your tongue
carried me on the bareness of your body
our skins murmured romantic fondles
smothered ourselves in the embrace
flamed our bodies to ecstatic convulsions
we melted in the fire of my losing virginity

Heart of the World

We live in heart of the world
the heart-shaped country
where sages did penance
for world peace,
chanted,
'let all beings, non-beings
live together in peace and harmony
a nation that contributed a full number
"Zero" to the world
Gandhiji lived here
a saint,
who Shook the British empire alone.

Only Hope and Bliss

I pray in my heart every day to fill and feel your presence. I
I kept an altar of love for you, a piece of my heart for you to play
My eyes are dry to cry anymore, let my craving for you never end.
Thank you, Lord, for letting me say an orison for the weeping whole
world.
You are my only hope and bliss, accept me as a prayer at your feet.

Magnanimity of Creator

Universe is stretching
beyond imagination
mind too is expanding
seeping into the unknown
in the vast expanse

many many galaxies live
then disappears into oblivion
there are many moons
many suns, millions of stars some are dead
some are light years away
their brilliance is yet to be seen

man thinks he is intelligent
conquered the cosmos
thinking of using planets as
dinner plates

imagine an ant seeing the world
his vision is limited to his sight
I wonder if I am an ant
my perception is limited
we are just a millionth of a spec
in the splendour of the universe
smaller than the smallest
attempting to be bigger than the biggest

if the mind can glimpse the vastness
knowledge dawns
wisdom rise
you feel humble, how puny, tiny you are
humility makes you bow down
at the magnanimity of the creator

# Door to Infinity

There is a door that opens to infinity
an ancient opening from time immemorial
it was there as ancient heritage in the mind
filled with the grandeur of grand images

the scenery outside changes often
but the onlooker absorbs the change of ambience
mountains, meadows, grooves valleys and streams
makes the scenic view different on seasons

often the moon stars and the entire sky fills
the drawing room of my mind, the breeze brings in
the fragrance of freshly bloomed flowers
the invigorating smell of nature makes me hum a melody

while writing about the summer smell from the courtyard
the smell of sacred Beel flowers seeps into my nostrils
Thank you my lord for keeping my senses fit
to become aware of the wonders of this universe
let me keep this admittance wide open for you always

Then That Too

One day I shall walk into
the flow of the Ganges.
I leave all my attire,
my adornments,
my sheaths,
my shrouds,
my ego and sorrow.
I never look back.
Maybe my remnants
will call me back.
I can hear them cry.
I said to myself
no turn back.
I watch myself
lifting by currents
my legs are off the bed
waves carry me
a little lamp afloat
streamed past
now high tides beating me.
I am engulfed.
in a surfing pool
my folded hand unfold.
I am at the mercy of the river.
suddenly tear everywhere
I gulp some water.

Some basal leaves
flow into my mouth.
A strong whirlpool ahead.
oh, she stretched her hands.
I merge in her embrace!
The floating wick- light
just flared up
then that too.....

Free Birds

We are all living,
on the tip of an iceberg,
floating in uncertainty,
moving along,
unaware of disintegration.

love birds,
they are in extreme love,
sitting on a ledge,
a hilt of time,
in serious discussion,
tweeting,
singing,
planning a home,
family.

sometimes
ignorance is a blessing too
living in the moment
you live
unaware of past and future
Free birds

A Designer Queen

She came with a heart full of love
when she smiled
a colour burst
tints of dust swept
creating butterflies
of every hue and shade
she became princess
a designer queen

Opera House

Star-studded azure sky sprinkles celestial light,
into the depths of cosmic dreams.
my eyes travel in a boat of imagination.
it is a glamorous glittering world of galaxies.
awestruck I wade into the fathomless sea of mystic mystery.
such tiny thoughts of mine sway in the mighty universe.
planets, in different constellations, live and exist,
respecting the pathways, who planned the entire solar system?
I wonder how a tiny bit of sand like me can conceive,
such a divine concept of these wonderful milky ways.
Oh my lord, my pen is inefficient to write anything of your drama.
let me live in your dream as a dreamy object a spec of stardust
oh if you had given me enough words
to describe your astounding magic Opera house! Lord.

Another Sapphire Sky

I wish to invite no one to read my verses.

But if my words beckon you by its grace,

It is a great honour for a man of no letters.

If it gives you the ecstasy of a fresh breeze,

then I am happy that I touched your heart.

If it sprays exotic fragrances around you,

remember it is your mind that emits.

If I retain a picture of my words in your heart,

I know you let me feather touch you by...

If any of my words echo and reverberate,

I know the muse lives in ever and ever.

Words flower as the sun in the sapphire sky!

Moon in Search of His Love

Moon glides over the sky
in search of his love
winking stars hide her among...
he treks through valleys of stars
climb cloudy mountains
Search the whole of galaxies
visited planets and black holes
he rode on meteorites
took the train of tailed comets

daily he beamed his searchlight
never could he find her anywhere
one day he spotted her
beyond galaxies across the milky way

he swam across
at last, he reached her
the entire beauty of the universe
had adorned her body
she had a crown of unique jewels
planets as gemstones

as he climbed the cliffs of desires
he put on a more golden hue
turning his body to purity
he rode on a horse of white puffy cloud
a full moon in romantic chivalry

they met under the flowing emotions
she covered him behind her hair
angels and fairies praised their love
time faded
sky raided
time to depart to reality
it will be daylight soon
birds started chirping from heaven

they parted
tears streamed as dew
the moon slowly shrunk into
a small piece like a bracket upwards
before turning into a back moon
next day he will start his journey again
to meet her! on the next full moon day
flooding with tides of emotion

Magic Show

A veil of mist still hanging on the eastern sky
behind the screen the green room is hectic
flint of the moon and faded stars beating the retreat
dress rehearsal is started, the head of the main actor moves
now the curtain is lifted
with soft steps, the magician appears
he lifts his cap and bows at the universe
soon a flutter of birds from his hat
he removes his tailed coat
a golden aura emits from his body
he turns his magic wand
thousands of golden needles flow
The Eastern sky is lit with a golden hue
every door and window is knocked
pouring golden glow of dawn
prayers rise from temples and churches
temple bells chime loudly
pigeons murmur and chant mantras.
they move around pecking at breakfast
the arrival of dawn mystifies the heart
children read their lessons loudly
light of hope glow on all faces
A new day opened its annals
the magic show continues until dusk

Small Me Too Big Me

What are some about me?
It is nothing but my meaning me
I mean me merges with the real me
become me of me
that is my real nature me
here my small me dissolves into a big me
I turn my universal
I fly high into realms of me knowledge
I become ecstatic me
me a floater on wings of freedom
I laugh and sing songs of devotion
my vision of myself changes
I turn into a mighty me
me of wisdom and me of knowledge
Do you know what is me in me?
it is truly me, the truth
me of pure bliss
me the purity
me of nameless me
formless me
timeless me
I remain in me as a tiny me too
a spec of light into full radiance

The Murmur of Skins

I need a dream
to delve into a fantasy
drenched in lust
I carry you
place you under
shower of my reverie
I foam your smoothness
fondling your excitement
we merged the aroma
of our body
sharing our wild images
together
we explored the
depth of night
searching ecstasy

we woke up
in each other's
embrace
listening to the murmur
of our sore skins
in the silence of
our lips

Sound of Silence

A crowd lives in the mind
stuffing with sounds and shouts
every single syllable is recorded
mind is stuffed, the brain is overloaded
aura is transcribed with desires
just listen to it to find; it's all delusions
a hoax created by an urchin
just live in the sound of silence
muteness shall speak louder than loudest

I Swatted a Fly

Somebody jumped off the balcony
a crowd is pooling around
fire force trucks have come and gone
police car screech to a halt
a no-entry ribbon around the place
crowd disperse one by one

with drenched mood
walked to the metro station
they are on strike
looked for a coffee kiosk
the flavour of Turkish coffee lingers
I swatted a fly
sipped potion
looking at dying fly

Angelic Firefly

Now everybody is celebrating
fade out of a wild black rose.
A celebrity of his rights
captured wide silver screens

Soon he became a black pearl
adornment in the starry sky
of the cinematic world in India.
like a comet, he flashed all over.
galaxies, singing loud folk songs.
created uniqueness in tune n tones.

Mani danced into every heart
with simple and soft steps of love
mimicked the reality of life around him.
filled the film world with his gigantic image
and acting skills by living in the roles.

leaving a trail of images in a golden hue
he left an angelic firefly.

He Fell in Love With His Painting

Every single stroke is a storyteller
bit by bit he created a lass in style
he filled his palette with silky thoughts
painted her in exquisite satin blue

the artist carved a piece of blue moon
placed it on his canvas as a monument
to add divinity to the expression
he painted his wife and son in silky blue

aesthetically he grew wild bloom
spreading the fragrance of his love
every leaf and each flower had his signature
he had his eyes planted in each shade
his canvas was manifesting the lord's colour
the azure sky twinkling with mystery
by watching closer to his painting

he fell in love with his graceful Wife

Just saw a contest prompt
Devotion
thought to write about it
then I saw a prompt picture
it was a woman's thigh
in black laced lingerie

what did I write?
erotica invaded wildly
picturized her
in secret vision
imagine
my prurience

Cloud of Memories

Between time and space
Lives a phantom of images
Split personalities stampede
Silhouetted by giant columns
Life gallops with a hoofing sound
I wonder who is the rider
Where is her destination?
I see meadow ahead,
And a carpeted floral terrain.
Mystical horse rider rides fast
Disappears in the cloud of memories.

I Found My Holy Temple

Worship by Vedic hymn
oblation of the idol
apply sandal paste on the body
don silky clothes adorn ornaments
gold and diamonds, gems and pearls
crown of Jewells.
apply perfumes and Vermillion on the forehead
sing a devotional song, drum and flute music
light oil lamps at the Sanctum Sanctorum
offer flowers, holy water light, incense, fruits
that completes the worship by offering five elements.
final offering burning of camphor
saying by not saying, nothing remains permanent
all vanish into nothingness
let my mind burn like incense
and spread the fragrance of love

My Holy temple is inside
I was inside worshipping my
personal God. Me

Six Pack Man

Out of a lump of shapeless disorder
I am deciphering my own identity
I was hidden behind filth of uneasy
time was holding my life breathe

then one day I struggled out of the mess
pulled my head up for dive up
slowly I realized the reason for my lose
I pushed up my will to struggle and stretch

My body is built out of ashes of time
like a phoenix, I rise from the grave of oblivion
now almost finished building my power pack
trying to shape my six pack v structure

Many come and watch me taking shape
they see me as a next-generation stone man
another spider man will incarnate soon
yew we shall meet an unaware fighting bad man

Highway to Destiny

An infinite pathway emerges from the
The window of history. It is a highway to destiny, and divinity.

Many great souls trekked this pathway
Placing imprints on their life.
Their footprints speak loudly,
For what have they done with their life for humanity?

The lantern they lit on the face of the earth,
Still, enlighten the track as an emotional,
The compassionate torch that guides.
Generations to generations to come.
Civilization to civilizations to arrive.
Let me pay obeisance by feeling their footmarks.

Originator

He created a world of his dream
Under the dim light of a lantern.
A magic world by a swift movement
Of his magic wand.
His world of wisdom reflects in his blue eyes
Many aeons have added grey,
In his luxuriant beautiful long beard.
A world of creativity rests under his hat
A great compassionate first-generation grandpa
A marvellous sculptor, of the universe.
Every small and big origin
Passed through his fingertips
Beauty and freshness rest in his thoughts
Each day he comes out with a new handcraft
A fresh thought, a fresh vision, a fresh aroma of life.
The originator of all aesthetic magic
When he moves his hand and says
Let the show begin, show beings
The show stops abruptly when he desires
The world is a magic show

Framed Blank Images

Running a painting exhibition.
Framed and hung my thoughts.
Wall was full of mind images
People knew I appreciated it.

Be a Shadow Until Then

An object is born with a shadow, a shadow is born with an object

Both are relative accordingly

A subject consumes an object, an object blocks a shadow.

Shadow eats away anything even a planet, planets eclipse to assume shadow too

This life is shadowed by a bigger object we relax in the comforts of bigger shadows and become shadows ourselves for many.

Better not to overshadow because you will be shadowing the comforts of light Belongs to all, be a shelter instead and protect from ultraviolet rays

Yes be a shadow for your child, until then

Utopian Word

I know nothing
Except that, I know nothing
I feel if I could
Discover one word
That was not used
As a concoctor of verses
I am just mixing
The words that are used
And lie dead
In the memory lexicon
Could I use one word
That is not stale, unused
And cover the
Entire universe
Like an ornated umbrella
If I come up with that word
I become a poem itself
Selling my myths, images
Smile, and imagery
My muse's crown would be
Adorned with the new Jewell
Of my utopian dream word!

At Your Mercy

You have a way
with your tongue,
way with your words
often that penetrates
to my heart.

You have a way
to comfort me.
I feel pretty safe
and secure
in your presence.

You could roll me
with a blanket
of your wisdom
where I turn mute
and remain
at your mercy!

His Story

A formatted dismantled
disk lie rusted
Once the motherboard
was active and running
pulses were good
bios too.
The signal moved in binary nerves.
Senses of sensors done well.
Memory chips
were functional,
inputs and outputs
were in standards.
Millions and billions
of files were at the tip
of function keys.

Then one day
thunder and
lightning struck,
power overshot
memory chips
and burnt battery.

Here lies my
friend dead
with a black face

and grin.
I dismantled and buried
his body in an electronic junkyard.

and kept his skull
as a souvenir
of my first laptop.
I wrote his story in my diary

With a Shy Smile

The mystery
to reveal shortly.
Behind the curtain
of darkness
a vein of flash
forms intermittently.
The stage is set
A canopy of light
hangs on centre stage.
Thousands of flowers
bloom instantly.
A spurt of flashing beams.
The Disco mirror globe rotates
Blaring scintillating music
Slowly a butterfly
zooms in.
She flapped her wings wider.
Her body flashed
few seconds
She lost her wings.
she was in a veil
of assorted lights.
A tune of the violin.
even that was gone.
On focused
flood light

Her sculptured body was
in the limelight for a few seconds.
Violent laser beams
tied and tagged her
she retires
covering her nudeness
with a shy smile.

A Day Retreats

Crystalline water
feels the shore
Ocean heaves, waves
moves in rhythm.
The sea has spread her
flowing dark blue hair.
A light breeze floats
through the crowded beach.
a litter of colours
in bikinis and swimsuits
loiter on the
recliner beach chairs
with a drink

The white sand is strewn
with footprints.
Kiosks are busy
with roaring business.
Stomachs full of beer
men lie on surfboards.
Waste bins are overflown
with empty cans.

Women in their
sunglasses look distantly.
Half-open book

lie on their flat belly.
Children shout
at their best voice.

Unnoticed a crab
was trying to reach the sea,
was pushed away
by the waves again and again

I took a last
look at the setting
sun
watching the
vermilion spread
slowly on shore.
A day retreats
into my mind

A Life Full of Hopes

Man lives
in the hope
of hopes
Hoping
from one to
another
Ending up
with hopeless
hopes.
Yet
hope
helps to live
in dreams
dear to
life
full of hopes

You Ignored Me

Where are you?
I shouted louder
No answer came,
echoed the same
question.

My mind was chatting
with me.
My thoughts
in disorder
I want an answer
an urge to know me
more.

I trekked mountains,
deserts, and forests.
Sailed seven seas
visited different lands,
looking for me.

No one guided me.
So I carried out a searchlight
flashing it everywhere,
I looked for me.
In my loneliness,
when aloofness

enveloped my mood,
I heard a sound,
You fool
why don't you
Search inside.
I am here
close to your heart.
I have been here
ever with you,
but you ignored
my signals!

Village Serene

No hurry
everyone goes with
the quietness of life
knows each other
Share
dreams, pain, sorrow
or happiness,
dance together.
Share live equally.
boys and girls
belongs to all family
old men are grandpas.

Village serene
where angels
visit daily

The Smell of Fresh Earth

The first drizzle
knocks at the windowpane
with pearly silky beads.
A thrill envelopes
body horripilate
Monsoon symphony
has begun.
Stretching hands
rubbing palms
I reach tiptoed
near the window.
the colours of
nature has changed.
The ambience is exotic.
The entire garden,
trees and flowers
swing in a dream.
the pathway is strewn with
flowers.

My heart jumps out
wish to dance
in the rain.
My body craves
for an aromatic shower
from heaven.

Body heat be
cooled.
Let freshness
fall on the skin.

Oh I love
the smell of
fresh earth
after rain.

Raising a hood of
hopes
serpents dance
I hold you in my embrace
and become
merged in the downpour.
we dance until
sneeze
wakes our body up
I wish my love to you
sprout again with vigour.

The Big God Lives

The big god lives
in a world of his own
Sarcastic protoplasm,
many parasites
suckle into the
enzymes for
power and prestige.

Many small gods
indifferent attired
assignments from
high command
roam and hover
over maggots
in the name of democratic
hypocrisy.
These demigods
collect blood money
and protection
handouts.

Often instigate
poor and desolate
in the name of

patronage of secularism
and return
to have their
last laugh.
when the riot
starts burning
the minds.

In the end the big one
arrives for a sermon.
An independence day speech
next
A republic day speech.
He throws
a torn quilt
to cover the faiths
and retreats
to his foreign
junket.

Long live the king
long live
democracy
The freedom
to Weep silently
is given to you
in abundance.
Freedom of speech!
that is all.

Expressions of Love

Escort you to the heaven of ecstasy
Make you the slave of my desires.
Floating on golden wings pruriency,
I suck every bit of your aromatic flow.
I swing my tongue elaborately over your privacy.
I can see your awestruck expressions,
making me madly in love making love.
We ride into the world of "Kamasutra"

The Scenery of Nature

Monet had to paint a lassie.
Vigorously he mixed colours
carved his vision on canvas.
Intricacies of a village belle.
He sketched the girl's dream too
As he stepped out for a puff of a cigar.
Listening to a brusque sound,
surprisingly found
that his painting had turned
into a beautiful scenery of nature,
emitting the fresh fragrance of life.

Fantasy Untold

Galaxy as a crown of glory
Beads of heaven cascade.
Her angelic wings studded
with silvery misty morning stars
As ravishing beauty cascade
she half opens her dreamy eyes.
Wearing a star-studded gown
she sprinkles pulchritude around.
Her half-opened roseate lips
utter a murmur of grace.
A rainbow colours her cheeks
becoming a dream in a dream.
She fizzles out as an aromatic mist.
a fantasy untold by time.

In Tune With Nature

Listening to music on earth
the gurgling stream of water,
underneath composes the life song.
I can see a pure crystalline water table
the lifeblood of earth and life.
The image of sculpting is created
by placing life being sensibly
as the silhouette of images.
Nature merges with life infusion
life blended with earth closely.
The creation of Dali breathes,
speaks sees listens to, feels and tastes.
A symphony of life in tune with nature

Kalidoscope

Beauty is created in the mind.
A tri-conical mirror bound together.
Body, mind, and intellect create a Kalidoscope.
Five senses nibble and place in
sounds, objects, tastes, smells and feels,
turning into radiant fractal images.
The mirror of the mind reflects and refracts
symmetrical fractal images in exotic designs.
spatial minds turn and twist infinitely,
builds patterns of wonder in space.
With an awesome expression
the face reveals nine expressions of life!

 Epithet

Write your
soul out
You will
hear
your sound
reverberate
everywhere
world
listens to
you,
your words
become
wisdom
epithet.

A Sandalwood Coffin

It has been quite a long time since I have been thinking to write about him. I am not sure how it will turn out, maybe a poem or a prose poem, no wonder if it stretches into a short story. Mathai chettan lives in a house in my village, about four blocks away. He was the headmaster and retired from a government high school. A straightforward and strict man with the ideals of Mahatma Gandhi, a freedom fighter too. He was an efficient English and Maths teacher. Often he boasts of many of his students at high places of power and prestige. Some of them are In civil service occupying positions of importance. Daily he used to take long morning walks and return with some, of his students following him in conversation with him.

He had his wife and four children two boys and two girls all were well-educated and married to decent families. They are all settled separately with their children and wives. The only sorrow he had was his children did not get into civil service or any higher positions. He often regretted it.

The story is not about that. Of late he had developed a hobby in woodwork. He used to work late at night in his workshop. A slow a rhythmic sound emanated from his compound. He did not allow anybody to his workshop and kept his unfinished work covered even his wife did not know about his secret sculpture.

Although he had his pension for his livelihood, his money had exhausted whenever his children visited him with demands and complaints. he made them happy by giving them whatever he could. Lately, he learned that his children are demanding to sell off his house. His wife also had no objection as she was a poor lady who loved them dearly and succumbed to their demands.

so the wise man decided to sell off his home on popular demand.

Since then he was busy in the workshop. One day he worked
late. The sound of wood coming out of the room had stopped
Master did not come out that day for his usual morning walk
surprised his wife went in to see him. Knocked, there was no sound of him
The door was ajar. wife peeped in, he was lying there, hands stretched
she ran to him. no sound of his breath. She found a note saying
"I am going, don't you worry about me. I have built a Sandalwood coffin
with artwork on it. Do not use it to bury me. Just hide it away from your
children. You will need this when your children will send you to an old
age home. Sell off the coffin, it will fetch you a good amount of money."
A plywood coffin is ready for me I kept nearby. Use it to bury me.
And goodbye, for now, we will meet again in heaven.

My Concocted Composition

I love to write with a pen.
Nowadays I do not
my laptop makes it easier
yet I keep a collection of pens
in different colours and shapes.

When an idea sprouts
I am very anxious
how my scribble turns out
Always I wanted her well dressed
wearing jewels of nine colours.
I write my poem anytime
night, day dawn, midnight
does not matter really.

I play with simple words
do now wish my reader
to use a cracker to my words.
whenever I look into the eyes
of my muse,
I like to see an ocean of images
waving and dancing in my mind
floating butterflies.
I like her to be bedecked
on a petal bed of my imagery.
I love her hide-and-seek play

that makes me explore her
elegance

Let me worship her
with scanty petals of my words
from the obscurity of my limitations.
Maybe would spend my whole life
in deep penance to invoke your grace
and see her amusing smile
for my concocted composition!

Bubble Burst

A star-studded dream
goes on making waves
to infinity

Unable to reach a shore
still, the ruffle moves on
creating
rounded curls on the surface
travels in space.

Innumerable galaxies
float beyond
umpteen light years away.

The roof of the circus tent
is lighted with
much much self-illuminating
stars and goblets
like a Christmas tree decoration.

Comets, planets, solar systems
milky way
Trapeze players
angels and fairies
the circus continues.
On the other side

a magician,
he controls the entire show.

Time square witnesses
the entire
equation E=MC2.

Time travels
from infinity to infinity
and reaches
eternity
then there
is no beginning
or end
that is the magnanimity
of mysterious
space.

Our mind conceives
all these wonders
like a dream
in the spec
of a thought.
A bubble
Inside out
and outside in!
That is a big bang
Bubble burst

A Withdrawal

When the sun appears
at the east
Dawn lifts its blanket
of darkness.
Raven retreats
to a black hole
in the sun.

In the pond,
a lotus opens
her eyes slowly
to full bloom.
She watches
the world with
dreamy eyes.

She invokes
the whole universe
into her soul
there it remains
outside in
and inside out
as macro
and microcosm.

The twilight
falls into the lap
of dusk.
Under the moonlit
serenity
she closes her eyes
shrinks
into meditation.
A withdrawal
in search of her soul!

A Colour Jam

She was strolling
in the garden
in slow and steady steps.

A sea of waves
in her deep blue eyes
a slow breeze was
curling her blue-black hair.

She was wearing
a floral gown
embossed with
exotically hued patterns
Her lips are half open
as if she is
making a wish
to the fairies.

A sudden wind
lifted her gown up
an effort to cover
herself
she leaned a bit.

Upfront
two moon faces
staring.
A hiss
a flutter of butterflies
off her skirt.
A colour jam
her skirt had
disappeared

Am I an Astronaut?

Oh my God
where am I?
I was having
my usual nap.
Am I dreaming?
How did I reach here/
Oh no I am
in a space suit.
I am seeing
stars, the moon
and planets
rolling
under a disco dome.
laser beams.
What are these dials
bleeping, hissing
Oh no there
is a big hand
coming up to my face!
It pushed my mouth open,
forced some good tasting
chicken legs. Yummy
Oh am I an
astronaut?

Drizzle of Hues

Witnessing scenario
of fast modern life
the city sky-kissers
stand erect
viewing
the drama.

When night
unties the bundle
of darned darkness
one by one
the street light
comes alive
pouring golden
helium down the
pathways.

People walk faster
on the sidewalks
to reach home early.

Unmindful
the city buildings
display and reflects
the scenes
live on the street.

Limousines honk
speed past the
glass houses
splashing
golden and silver
streaks of light
leaving
an impressive
drizzle of hues.

Dreaming Woman

Pulchritude cannot be
explained but experienced.
The abundance of my love
flows to you incessantly
as a sigh of longing lust.
I want your body and mind
to hold my pruriency
like a tentacle rooted
in your soul filling me
with the sensual dream of
overflowing fulfilment.
You are a playboy of
my womanhood

Aurora

The night ends at the tip of a cliff
where the moon still meditates.
A flood of golden hue awaits
behind the mountain range.

The serenity of nature cascade
falls on the lap of the valley.
Time pauses for a moment
to absorb the exotic ambience.

Behind the dawn of freshness
the chant of hymns arise
greeting the morning sun
Chant of Gayathri purifies the air

Priests and saints take the holy dip
In the river of purity
the holy fire-offering, the fragrance of incense
temple bells chime welcoming
the divine grace falling on earth.
Putting some words of aurora
I light a tiny wick at the feet of the world

Silent Prayers

I just want to live here
for a while until.
Let me obscure
far from the madding crowd.
Pray let me
take little from
mother nature
become part of her
give my heart.
Let my breath do not
pollute her.
Just enough water
a hand full of morsel
floor bed
soulful song
silent prayers
from the depth of my heart
To invoke Lord

Gloamings
 All leave this world empty.
Some get out emptied.
Most left accumulated.
Even a beggar dies rich.

Great men lived here
casting a divine shadow
of his life over society
it was their ideals that
we made idols of worship.
Those silhouettes are our
uniting force, shadows of hope.
We protect those ideas.
A great wall of hopes
lets us live in the coolness
of summer heat waves.

We named it isms, religions.
Those are the gloamings
that secure our worldly life.

Frilled Thoughts

A golden thread
moves through the shuttle
weaves a handloom poetry.
The poet is in a trance
pushing the weft in rhythm.
Soft floral designed silk
stretches out of Weaver's
imagination with floating
imagery and lively images.

The poet never rests
his pen scripts the creation
from his magic hat.

A cute white rabbit jumps out
runs in the minds excitingly.
The weaver rests his head on the loom
dreaming the brightly woven silk.
The poet withdrew his pen
talking to his words in silence.
He lifts his colourful wings
waving and weaving in ecstasy
his frilled thoughts lie scattered.

In the Solitude

Sun peeps
through the lips of time
holding a
diamond ring
to pass through a kiss
to miss Moon.

The picturesque
beach
is witnessing
the lover's
deep love,
their long sigh
invoking
hopes for tomorrow.
Weaving a dream
together
in the solitude
of ecstasy

Beauty and Brain

If I had enough words to adorn her
enough imagination to adore her.
Maybe I would be knighted with a smile
a poet of the royal court of Cleopatra!

More than, a queen she was a woman
who was graced with beauty and elegance
a flaming beauty tickled and tricked men.
She was a unique creation of the lord
well carved in a ravishing sculpture
in flesh and blood.

Despite her beauty, she had a shrewd brain.
Like a spider, she trapped the Roman empire
made Julius Caesar and mark Antony her prey
made a puppet show of their life!
She tied and entangled them in her silky web
trapping them on her bed of desires.
opened her womanhood
became the virtual queen of Egypt and the Roman Empire.
She was a torch
Then became a flame
Then a battlefield
And a towering inferno
that consumed herself
in the Venum of the feud
and cruelty.
Entire rich Roman empire!
disappeared in her witchcraft

Fragrant Words

Yes, the word takes birth
and never dies.
She lives forever beyond aeons.
It is recorded in the brain,
in digital forms, in the aura,
in the air it floats, in thoughts, it lives
in sound waves, it dances.
lively in music
The imagination of a great muse
makes it flower
aesthetically in poets
it is fragrant too.

It is a dream that
humans live in.
in the silence of its
manifestation.
Unique
wonder that is ever created
by the merciful Lord!

Fondest Memories

Remember
we are just two
passengers on a train journey.
Never knew we meet
yet we met.
travelled together
shared all we had
slept in our arms of dreams.
Every dawn and dusk we saw
through the windows.
Seasons, we watched
together.
carry me
in your
fondest memories
darling

Spark of Love

Can I give you a fathomless kiss, that will make you sigh
if only you can see my passion, will that make me entwined
if the sky remains forever will the love too also your elegance
come to me my girl and let the life flow never close your hopes
never let the dream goes astray
let your heart knows that my heart is with you in the good and bad
times
don't say ever no, but take my hand, will you?
see in my eyes that divine spark for you will never die even after I die

Stillborn

Silence speaks volumes
words are pregnant
with meanings
but what is the
use of meaningless
meanings
just to deliver
a stillborn baby?

What Are We?

Day mates with night
producing twilight.
The sun meets the moon
producing
Star children.
Stars grow to megastars
living in
ivory towers.
Some live far
light years away.
They never shine
in the horizon.
Some are shooting stars
in a galaxy of Western classics.
Some live in the elegance
of beauty and purity.
Some are comets
burning away.
What are we? stardusts?

Love-Filled Tears

What are we?
All in one
Waiting for sunshine
Spark of love

In the solitude
Dancing with souls
caressing my thoughts
soulful images.

Unexplored
steams of desires.
The day I was born
to carry a dream.

World is a drama in a dream.
Unwritten poem
unfathomed ecstasy
caressing my thoughts.

Fragrant words
aesthetic purity
in the lake of clarity
an abundance of elegance.

To melt my anxiety
echoes from bamboo.
Symphony, silent prayers
love-filled tears.

Your Kindness

Mother Earth is out
planting the paddy field
with her own hands.
She wears the beauty of the mud
the smell of lively earth.

We the babies looking
for her grace
hoping her feed of life.

Winter or rain
she is there at dawn
watching her plants grow
weeding and feeding with manures
while her baby is fed
with her breast milk.

Life lies ahead like
a smooth clean sheet of water
Oh, Mother thank you
you are the one
who feed us with the best
of your love.
How can we ever return
your kindness
with equal abundance?

Invisible Painter

Invoking the subtle magic of dawn
she stared at her blank canvas and easel.
had emptied her mind and thoughts,
then filled it with colours of nature.
Drew colours of the rainbow,
golden hues of the morning sun.
shades of retiring moon and stars.
She mixed every paint in her palette
squeezed out of her imagination.
Mixed a mixture and life and death in an exclusive dye.
Had her brush bristle made of sun rays!
Invisibly she drew the tinge and elegance of nature.
Her unique brush sprayed unknown pigments,
in her empty canvas and drew the aroma of nature.
The white canvas was full of an exotic picture
It was a blush of the invisible painter
The painter signed " I am not"

Drain Me Dry

Floating on waves of desires
I wished I could be near him
for once more.

I wish to get lost in his manliness
in the wilderness
of his strength.

His pounce is expectedly near
prowess on his prey
ready to succumb
to the power of the master.

I sense his first kiss
draining away my lips,
then my emotions.
My lust
My pruriency
he will eat me as a slave
pouring his sweat and love
making my soul drench
in the downpour
of his lovemaking.
My lust is wandering
for his solace
Oh, love to drain me dry

Self-realization

There was a traffic block in the numerals, nine was blocking the flow
an obscure Indian saint put a roundabout, oh, the move of numbers
made smooth, great Inventor of the time. there are six centres of power
aligning the function of body mind and intellect, Plexes of energy
The root chakra, sacral chakra, Solar plexus, Heart chakra, throat
chakra,
The third eye is the crown chakra. sixteen syllables powerful mantra
of Tripura Sundari. There are five organs of action, five senses, and five
life breaths, and then the body, mind, and intellect add to eighteen.
Ultimate realisation comes
with a bang of effulgence. Eighteen is double Nine as well
A Tunnel to the Truth
 Five senses on retreat.
Retired into the pool of tranquillity.
From the mighty depth,
a spring of purity sanctifies
the pool of imagery.
a little circle of images rest
on the shore of serenity
high beam of light
from the whirlpool of effulgence.

I wonder who can create
such images,
which talks to the soul.
The mighty brush strokes
deciphered and dug
a tunnel to the truth.
An escape root for the
jailed senses of life

Graffiti of Life

With a mix of bits and pieces
of confetti collected from
the sun drops
I mixed in my palette
a unique combination
of a magic pigment.

I went on to create a painting
of my soulful images.
On the face of the horizon

I painted graffiti of life sketches,
it had the hue and brilliance
of a rainbow.
Often I glided and played
like a little boy
with thrill and wonders
of a beginner.
Come join me in the
exploration.
I shall carry you to my dreamlands
of fantasy

My Prayer Will Not Be Complete

You gave us the earth as food, gave bliss of light for the sprout of hopes. Streamed yourself as spring of love, Filled your lungs with sweet fragrant air.

We live under the blanket of your warmth. Sleep fearlessly under the roof of the azure sky. decorated with stars, moon, sun, and planets. But we did nothing for you Lord. Instead, we destroyed everything you gave and jailed you in the cages of our greed. crucified you for a pound of greed and crowned you with our sins

Time Puts a Crinkle

Baby blooms
turn vibrant
fragrant flower.
youngster
with colours
sprinkles freshness
showers love.
Seasons
changing
ambience.
When the tree rains
flowers fall
faded
petals.
time
crinkles
the face of Life

Although, I Am Tired

Although, I am tired
It is just one more minute
I shall be done with.
But I can't sleep anytime
because I have no time.
My body is melted
dripping and wounded.
A surreal Dali clock
is kept on a line
to dry.
Temperature is low
yet, I have to display
my hour

Time river is flowing
incessantly.
A Bubble is floating
with a measurement
of hours and seconds.
That is me.
When I burst into the stream
another time machine
will float
until then
watch me as watch!

Unwritten, Undiscovered Lines

Unwritten, undiscovered lines
still adorn you
in every colour and hue
words and thoughts
sprang from your soul.

In a garden of
intricately carved
images and simile
you rule as queen
sitting on a thrown of
sounding syllables.

With an empty pen
and mute mind
I wait for your smile

Candle of Love

On a day of reminiscence,
we place
colourful bouquet for the
coffin underneath the tomb
we pitchfork and heap
delightful thoughts about him
soulful memories
of his deed
he is the solace
when the time
is bad
his epitaph read
"I love rattlesnakes too
light a candle of love
for them"

Into the Abyss

The Earth sounds
Rhythm of life
Just listen silently
Serenity arrives slowly
Entire macro dance
Under dreamy bliss
Your breathe stops
As you meditate

The wind looks
Through the passage
Time gallops fast
Leaving behind all
Unfolding my mind
I look back
The beaten path
awestruck I wait

The rain tastes
The sweet memories
Drizzle of purity
Flames of desire
sprouts in mind
I hug wilderness
to become mature
to drench me

The fire smells
Embers in ashes
words turn flames
Infuses the powers
Blazes lick mind
Burns the impurities
Slowly serenity dawns
forms the infinity

The Mind feels
beyond the sky
Entire galaxies cascade
As tiny drop
In my vision
I dive deep
Into the abyss
Of eternal truth.

A Kiss of My Wish

There was a girl
living in my soul.
She often tickled
me in my loneliness.
often mocked at me
in my daydreams.
She caressed me
in my thoughts,
teased me,
making me angry.

Then she consoled me
with a warm hug of love
kissed my imagination
leaving a lip mark
on my cheeks.
I thought of bringing
her out to paint her image,
a model for my portrait,
but she was shyly elusive.

One day when
she was very lively
in my imagination
I invoked her with
a magic brush

montaged her
with attributes
of her naughtiness.
I made a glowing
flowing, chatting picture!
I put my soul
as pearl drops on
earlobes, A kiss of my wish!
I put her name
"Pearly my dream"

On a Special Day

On a special day like this, Grandma, you lit your first birthday candle
with your little mouth blew it making an innocent wish for
the uncle moon in your courtyard.

You grew up the sprinkling charm
for Mom and dad, every moment.
showered merriment in their heart.
Became a little star adorning their simplest of wishes.
Showered you with all the best they could buy for you
Time moves fast, many seasons arrived,
filling your life with pulchritude.
you turned into a Venus gracing with glow and glamour around
became a dream of young men

One day you found your heartthrob, you wedded Grandpa
then both of you sailed in the ocean of life together
with swiftness and care.
Grandpa at the wheel you navigated,
have passed through many rough kinds of weather,
yet your boat sailed smoothly, your children grew up in your
warmth and comfort.
Sun, moon and stars guided you through.
Your prayers were answered by the lord by guiding you through time
you did not know eighty years have passed
Oh my grandma Mary Elizabeth Maynard Gaddi
I baked this cake for you with the Dough of love.

It is sweetened with sugar of respect,
decorated with nostalgia and creamed with bondage
I light the candle with prayers for your
health and happiness forever and ever

The Macho Man

The macho man just relaxes
in the cool of his wilderness
he lay spread in the vastness
with the beauty of his hot body

he conducts his heat in each grain of sand
flexing his muscles far and wide
rolling his biceps to a heap of power
stone built up of a six-pack monster

under the scorching manly sun,
he lies spread suntanning his body
the wind-swept body shelters many
his camel of desires steps into his mind slowly

images in his mind float as wild animals
in the chill of the night, he lets
the moon and stars sleep under his glow
he is a romance with many Oasis wives

when wild animals slip into fields
he gets up as a storm of the desert
rising dunes as he turns and twists
nobody can ignore him with disrespect,
He is the man! only man, only man.

Bonfire of Your Care

I see you through the mist,
dancing on a holy land of mystery.
From the hell of the time
I found you rescuing, salvaging lives,
placing them nearby the bonfire
of your care and warmth of love.
I watch the elevated souls
floating on the wings of effulgence.
With awe and wonder, I look at you
hoping for your benevolence for my salvation.
I lift my little hands in prayers,
so help me God help me God.

A Canvas of Grace

I am sketching my thoughts
in black and white.
Yesterday I had a dream at the dawn
I heard your sweet song.
from a golden cage of bondage.

I wish to hear your open voice
unrestricted by time and tide.
Let it be my song of love
You are free my bird
Flutter your wings to infinity,
into freedom.
Move into a dreamland
I draw my freedom strokes
for you.
Release you from my heart
to the mighty canvas of gracefulness.

Poets Are Strange Beings

POETS ARE STRANGE BEINGS
With a soul full of words,
mind full of thoughts,
heart full of love,
he was looking for her.
Trekked length and breadth,
by searching eyes.
Wondering where she is?
A bag filled with his loin clothes,
he moved from city to city,
village to village.
Turning himself as seasons
Met many women,
Lived in, cuddled by them.
Figured and hatched by their warmth.
Ultimately he wrote many poems.
Floating himself on a lotus boat,
filling it with petals of his heart,
soft, rose lotus petals.
The emitted the fragrance of his love,

he left each of his women,
by making a poem of his love.
Intoxicated by the unique aroma,
of their body and hair oil.
He wrote divine verses of passion.
Left; leaving a candy box for his children.
Trekked with a rubber soled boot
to the land of unknown

The World Is Beautiful

She is beautiful with a smile
at her dark nose.
Look at her flowing white
hair on her cheeks,
so glamorous and elegant.
There is a victory mark on her forehead,
showing a sense of wisdom.
She has a dream so dear
and fantasy of life too!
I wonder what she is looking for
A doggy's day out?
or a wild chase for her prey?
or a handsome Doberman?

She is cute and beautiful,
like a Barbie in Flesh and Blood.
Her eyes dream of stars and the moon
her face is moonlit,
waiting for him,
There is a peacock dance
in her eyes, the dance of love
with exotically coloured
blue and green quills
move in rhythm to the tunes of rhapsody!
The World is beautiful, So beautiful

Golden River

The golden moon was to fall
Caught him in my palm
He smiled and fizzled out
Melted, dropped off between fingers
Flowed smooth a golden river.

Dance Floor

My window opens to
infinity, into the wonders of
magical universe.
My window with a view
is my connection to
the eternal wonders of
the sky

I keep my heart open.
Daily, stars look into my eyes,
talk in silence with a wink.

We often dance in our thoughts.
I hold their hands
soft shiny hands.
Moon often gives me
his charming smile of
comfort.
I grab him in my dreams
adore him with
a glow of my love.

The entire cosmos
is on a disco floor,
dancing the night out,
celebrating.
The sum at the centre
with a flooding beam.

The milky way
cascades into my
courtyard.
I swim and swing
In ecstatic strokes.

There Is No Time

If in eternity.
I want nothing.
I lost everything.
Even my entity.
My identity was also lost.
But you know what
I have everything
the entire universe
and galaxies
the planets, the moon, the stars,
entire planetary systems
are mine!

When everything
is at my disposal
what should I need?
I will just be me
embracing the world
with love and compassion.
and all are mine.
Just one family
all belong to me
belong each other
so what we need
since there is
no beginning or end
There is no time sense!

I Love to Be Here

Hesitantly I came in
in silent steps.
Not to disturb the great poets
in their poetic workshops.
The Hall of Fame is
decorated with the
profiles of unique creators
of poems and artworks.

The hall is lit tastefully
focusing and floodlighting
on the dedicated writers.
I found it looked like a mural
of United Nations,
aiming in creativity
of the world of letters.

Awestruck I look at them
with reverence and wonder.
Great master poets live here
their grey-bearded wisdom
sprinkles the aroma of poetry.

I wondered what am I doing here.
to match with these giants.
I have only a feeble quill
and scanty vocabulary.

In the obscurity of timidness
I pulled out a verse from my heart
and submit at the feet of magnanimity.
Oh I am happy to be here
with my scribbles.
And it is being resonated
in my hollow-drum
I often beat it disturbing the serene
minds of ladies and gentlemen poets
who bear with my urchin mischiefs.
But I love to be here
feel the fresh air
and fragrance of life!
I love to be here

A Piece of Sky

We stole
sliced
a piece of sky.
It is bleeding
bit by bit.

The sky falls down
through
the ozone hole.
Catastrophe
results in
a cave in
of meteorites.

Planets tumble.
The sun takes a dive
with his flamy face
burning the earth.
Forest fires
acid rains.
Ultimately
a tornado hits
bleeding the earth,
burning forests.
holocaust of
ultraviolet blossoms
on the skins.

It is the nature's
eyes
that bleeds
through the lips.
Still vampires
are rising
from the graves
Let us fix a cross
of conscientiousness?

A Country Wedding

Plantain leaves lie scattered on a corner.
Black ants are having a feast from the remains,
Make a beeline out into the coconut groove.
With a grain of morsel each on their head.
Stray dogs are growling, and snarling, their teeth out,
Threatening each other, ready for a fight,
Crows are calling their friends, for a share of the meal.
A crowd is flocking in, pecking at the remains of a marriage lunch.

The guests are leaving one by one,
Some stand, in a circle, gossiping.
Chewing Beatle leaves, with lime and betel nuts.
Often, spitting thick red saliva on flower plants.
Some men are enjoying a rare cigarette smoke,
Peculiarly holding the cigarette under their fist.
Looks on as if they are doing a wonder!
The village head is encircled by a few admirers.
Showing off the nuptial poem he wrote for the occasion.

Women in silk Saris giggle and murmur shyly.
The back of their blouses was smeared with hair oil,
Makes a dark shade, mingling with perspiration.
Their lips were in red hue leaving a drop or two of-
-Beatle juice on their chins.

Children having the whale of a time.
Playing hide and seek, with their pals.
Slowly the drummers left, their drums,
Covered, in khaki clothes hung on the shoulders,
Stops, in front of a pinch of tobacco.
The caterers depart carrying empty pots.

Suddenly, the crowd huddles together on the porch.
The floral-decorated car arrives,
The driver moves out, taking pride in decorating the car,
Combs his hair looking at the rear mirror.
The groom cracking jokes with his friends walks in.
The bride arrives, in her beautiful braided sari,
Wearing, all her Jewellery, her hands covered in bangles.
The old men and women assembled in order.
Blesses, the newly wedded, as they touch their feet,
While placing some money on a Beatle leaf.
Suddenly, the girl sobs as she embraces her mother and father.
It's time to say goodbye, as the auspicious time approaches.
All lift their hands gesturing good wishes.

The great-grandma sits on the floor, legs stretched.
Slowly starts to grind the Beatle leaves with the ingredients
The slow and rhythmic sound from her small mortar
Mixes in her thoughts, and takes her back to her time.
She was thirteen when she got married!
She often opens a small box, and inspects a flower,
she had kept from her wedding bouquet.
It had lost its freshness too, dry as her thoughts!
Colourless as her skin.

Stampede of Time

I timed back in a time
met me in the twilight.
Was squeezed out of
a time machine.

My body had been
changed young
Had dark hair and a beard.

I was puffing a cigarette
waiting for my tram.
The scenery was
in black and white.
My vision was bright.

I was in Calcutta.
Suddenly came
a procession of protesters.
The scenario was
independent struggle.

Outside the square
an explosion
the governor's cavalcade
was bombed
viceroy escaped
the blast.

The black and white car
lie wounded
reminiscents
the stampede of time.

My Stillness Is My Poem

When I write a poem
It is a dream come true.
From the silence of the mind
from the deep slumber of thoughts
I discover a word, an image,
or a soulful feeling of glitter.

I invoke the source of silence
investiture on a high pedestal
I worship the image,
offering all the best of enchants
adore it with a rhythm.
I add a simile like a bloom of a flower.
Idolise my emotions
by consecrating with words
of oblation.
Add rhythm and rhymes
by tuning into my heart.
My emotions flow out
from a pen inked by the grace of the muse.

I take a snapshot of the scene
with an inner eye of love.
Here comes a passionate picture
from the magic hand of the unknown.
The poem is not mine as soon as it is on paper

I took it unaware from
an aura of past, present and future!
Don't worry my poem is silly.
My silliness is my poem!

"I Am Unique in That I Know"

"I am unique in that I know"
I know nothing uniquely
whatever I know is already known
crammed, stuffed knowledge
When you know the real
You will fall into the volume of silence
No more for this pen
No more tongue-lash
I live in the sui generis obscurity

Animal Planet

What dad is doing upstairs?
Is he watching animal planet?

Tsunami

Only yesterday all the birds were chirping happily,
waiting for the spring season, their hatchlings thrilled.
Excited animals roamed freely in the woods invigorated
by fresh and fragrant air. music of the earth rises in the air
to the tune of cosmic rhythm. Life was ticking from every corner.
Fresh bamboo shoots sprout
Sea waves were dancing heaving in excitement.

Yesterday it was not like this, a sudden a chaos
The birds stopped singing. Dogs and cats ran for life.
It was raining cats and dogs all day and night.
Mountainous sea waves rise high above coconut trees
Deluge engulf tall buildings and threw away ships ashore.
automobiles float without a rudder.
yesterday the ocean was peaceful and calm.
Now it retreated far into the outer realms
Anger and hunger of nature manifest as the tsunami.
Yesterday it was not like this, the flow of music from the flute was
ecstatic

Why?

She had followed me
all the way
as a dream.
Was in her
wedding gown.
Cuddled
in the boot of my
thoughts,
a fantasy,
I carried her in my heart.
As fantom of hopes
One day I found her
dead in my imagination.
Why?

Gets Energized by Gossip

Dawn to dusk
I have been washing dirty linens all day.
Don't you see I have a life too to live?
I can't take it anymore
Those ladies are chatting incessantly.
Don't they see my tongue out?
craving for a chat, although I am tired.
like any lady I have
a right for gossip
when I am exhausted.

Queen of Darkness

The queen of darkness
retreats to
an island of
remoteness.

Delves
deep into
meditation
to rescue
souls from
the abyss of sin.

when she closes her
eyes,
world
sinks into nightfall

Awakened
She sends her raven
with a flint of
light to
enlighten
sun.

Toughness is the Theme

Toughness was the theme
when men were chasing gold
invading settlements with fire
Fire liquid and firepower

They tamed wild horses
became grouchy bad-tempered
mounted on the beasts
rode on them faster than the wind

these wild horses loved
their mean masters
like a desert storm
became part of the desert life

both men and stallions
moved with hard climate
resisted winter and heat
roasted lizards for lunch
rattlesnakes for dinner

all men went to the west
in search of gold mines
they ploughed every land
plundered even burial places of the Reds

contaminated lives of Native Indians
fought battles with chieftains
sided with Apaches and Comanche
moved with desperados and mercenaries

The theme of cowboys evolved
becoming storyline for movies
for songs and culture
part of the history of the human race

Serene Tune

Unaware mind
babbles
biting the tongue
donning hatred
and venom
of insinuation.

All the time
all the efforts
for suppression of
the hood of ego
meets with
rejection and dejection.

Anger and frustration
compels
an attempt
to be you
without a mind
unpolluted.

Your prayers
are answered with
a sonorous
soft serene tune
emitting from a flute

from the lips
of the Lord.

You are snake charmed
into the basket of
compelling
compassion.

Beyond the Garden of God

Beyond
Garden of God
beyond
dead sea
and mountain
ranges
behind
veil of mist
mistic
mystery
manifests
in life forms
everywhere
in flowers
fruits
and on every
beings and
non-beings

I See Love

I see love

in your eyes

I can see

you anxiety

you waiting

for your beloved

I hear your sigh

your

excitement

prospects

of seeing the beauty

everywhere.

I sense you

your sensual thoughts

your love lust.

It is written

on your

face

LOVE

A Bit of an Illusion

An end to all is the truth
the truth will never end
in any fire, ice or deluge.
but matter ends to appear
in another form another time
there is one substratum
that withstands floods of delusion
A piece of peace is lost
in a matter of confusion
The reality of entropy is
at work in a v bit of an illusion

Last Supper

Unconcerned she was relaxing.
The cage of her fate was staring at her.
She did not know she was sitting duck.
Cruel bait for a leopard,
who was having a pleasure hunting?
When the village dives into a deep slumber,
He stole chickens, goats and other pets.
The Forest department was waiting for him,
with juicy prey of a dog.
But, who answers the prayers of a poor dog?
Look at her she sits there wagging her tail,
as gratitude for a sumptuous supper.
Last supper?
"Oh, my poor little puppies where are they?"
Did they get something to eat?"
She remembered her siblings.

Note:-

Recently it was in the newspaper that the forest department
was trying to capture a leopard who was running loose in the villages
disturbing the peace of domestic animals and villagers, hence this poem

Hunger

There is a party going on, a full-course dinner party
Up in the haven of the starred hotel There, guests arrive with a whim
a bash to celebrate dieting, Of course, they are living to eat there
and starving to live, abundance is their hunger so they starve to eat
more

Down in the waste bin at another party,
a party of the hungry and hunger
it is a place for all who want a morsel the cats, dogs, the beggars
and all creatures.
it is a buffet dinner eaten on the same plate
the difference is they are eating to live, starved to eat.
Hunger lives in them as a course n' curse of time.
Their faces are shadowed by the pain of helplessness

I wonder if there could be a world without
any starvation at least for one day!

Because I Found Him

I have been a doll,
beautiful Barbe doll.
Like princess
I appeared
in the newest
of designer outfits...
Was a model.

Children adorned me
in their fantasies, and dreams.
Men admired secretly
searched,
my real model.
Women were jealous

I am at a low ebb now
was heartless,
a rigid frigid female.
I want to darn my heart
filled with feelings
of a whole woman, sexy, sensual,
sentimental and sensational Barbie!

My Half Fullness

My half-full glass tells to the half emptiness that, were you not full once when you emptied yourself to fulfil my half of fullness.?

At Your Doorsteps

The smell
of you soul
spreads
though
your silence.
World
arrives
at your
doorsteps

Poet Is Just a Ploy

Poetry is a snapshot
of a moment
through the eyes
of a pen
flashed with words
backed
by images of the time.
Framed
with the elegance
of metaphors
and simile,
finely tuned with meters
and rhyming
Poet is just a pen of God

Droplets of the Night

The golden crown of the sun
fell at the feet of darkness.
Large winged black butterflies
flew away Heltar- skelter.
The earth was covered in a hail storm
My body was tattooed with
dark zebra butterflies.
Hailstones melted dripping
the heart of my angels.
I flew away on my wings of despair
draining my sorrow
through the eyes of the night,
leaving dark droplets of the night
on flower buds of sorrow.

Unaware of the Day and Night

A fog just spreads in the eyes
The greyness of gloomy surroundings.
The world had fizzled out of view.
Rainbow vanished into oblivion.
The glow on the face faded

In a world of confusion,
they remain unconfused.
Remaining above the time
they tie a knot to the past.
Live in each moment as a stranger
to the day-to-day life.
In a present world of their own,
unaware of the ambience and sceneries.

For them, the world just
gets dissolved each second
then starts again in the next minute.
Do not see the sun or the moon
as they live in the infinite effulgence of time.
Unaware of day and night.

Great exponents of their chosen field
they become masters of unique sculptures,
so elegant and beautiful,
that we look at them awestruck.

The world knocks on their minds
but they rarely open up.
when out of the cocoon
they show artefacts they spun
from the time
with silky threads of aesthetics.
They live on this earth as idols of God
God's children true replicas of the lord.
But for them, the world is an excursion!

I Fell off the Pocket

I fell off the pocket
of a superstar who
made me cling
with a quarter.

I was his lucky coin
worshipped by him

Yesterday I jumped off
to freedom.
Nobody cared
The sun shines for you.
Come on pick me up
Make your me icon.
I will bring good luck.

Thoughts in Disarray

The lake stands still
like a sheet of glass.
Beautiful silvery and golden
fishes swim engaging.
The lake bed is clear
clean underwater ambience.
Bubbles bugle through
fishes come out splashing.
Suddenly a ripple
the lakes turn into
a turf of active waves.
Somebody pelt a stone
it skips over the surface.
The moon fades out.

Lumps of dirt fall over
the water gets dirty.

Turbulence in and out.
The mind gets stirred
a flash of lightning
and lightwaves skim through.
Sudden leap of a frog
into infinity.
Thoughts in disarray
spit out wildly off the tongue.

A murmur of the lake
in shrill voice echoes.
from a faraway distance
The frog lies pinned
on a board for tranquillity
he will be barbequed soon!

Spirits in Him

Spirits in him
hugs his spirit.
He stands erect
while the floor
dances around.
Chivalry wakes up
as a Superman,
ready to fly off the roof.
Whistling a song
tapping on the floor
he leaves the bar.

Head reels.
The illumination
blind eyes,
with mashed lights.

With a full bottle of scotch
he retires on a bed of
glass splinters and vomit

Valour of Humanity

Honour me with
my rights as
a human.
Let me walk tall
with the valour
of humanity,
and love as
Medallion

Ready to Melt Any Time

From the unknown fathoms of time,
Millions and millions of years back
I was formed as a tiny drop of water.
Transcended me into a frozen mass
Of ecstatic happiness to freedom.
I never bothered to measure my depth
Yet am floating as a time block ready to melt

Musk-deer

From the universe of dreams
I step out.
as a unique articulation of grace
spreading the fragrance of musk.
I just want to manifest my image
all over your dream,
floating in the sky,
walking over the sea.
Just live as musk-deer
intoxicating you with
the aroma of musky sensuality.

Let me flow into you as a mist
to fill you with rapture.
Carry you as prince and princess
to a new world of magic
mound on my back
to ride to a world of fantasy,
the seventh heaven of your imagination.

Monocycle

You have to have some balance.
As a toddler, you move to fall and fall to rise.
Legs are balanced to walk.

When the ear balance was broken you again fall.
You are chemically imbalanced
Then balanced by medicines.

Body tranquil is kept by the spine
steady to go up again.
As you live in this world
need a mental balance.
With the mental and physical equilibrium
communication takes place,
In sound words and legible sounds.

From a clean mind, clear and clever thoughts arise.
Once put together all senses are in line
you become a man and woman integrated.
world gets unbiased.
One can stand on the feet, ride a bike, bicycle, horse or car.
Our axle will not be broken.

Living in the world is a balancing act
between good and bad
Existence in the reality of duality is important.
Until one can ride a monocycle!

Let Me In

I do not know
what am I looking for
with a long
tickling tongue.
Maybe an entry
to your soul
I have my tongue print
On you
as an id card.

I Have a Song to Sing

I have a soaked heart
filled with pulchritude.
My thoughts flow as a crystal stream.
While on its journey
I caress both banks
feeling and touching lives all around.
Dive deep into the fertile soil.
Regenerate seeds to sprout.
I visualised a whole new world,
kicking and spreading.

I listen to each syllable
each sound, each word,
that sprouts in my heart.
I spill it on paper
Is it my poem, No it is my life.
My experiences.

Then again the million-dollar question
why do I write?
then I ask myself
Why do birds sing, It has a song to sing.
I have a song to sing!

Symphony of Rain

There is a symphony going on.
The frog is the conductor of the baton.
Crickets crock on their high pitch,
while little frogs control the rhythm.
Up in the trees, bluebirds sing
The raindrops tap dance on rooftops,
with rippling rhyme and rhythm.
The cascade of streams falls as the chain of beads
the earth gets a face wash
with an aromatic drizzle.
Seeping darkness gives me hopes
of a celestial downpour through a sieve.
I love the moody rainclouds assemble
at my backyard with a glow.

I love watching the rain with a meditative mind
it invokes the exquisiteness of nature in me.
I Raindance under the canopy of rain,
get drenched in the holy water from heaven.
Monsoon gives me the prospect of a dreamy night
embraced wildly with enchantments
I love floating, walking dancing in the rain
smell the fragrance of fresh earth,
get intoxicated by, drinking the pour of Ambrosia

Just a Funny Poem

Wonder is maiming catastrophes
Donald Duck waiting at the gate
Trump is tramping the destiny of Hills
A black stallion is all she wants
When I have Clintons in my backyard
I need not worry about Obama
you can have a concise dictionary
North Koreans and Iranians chickenfeed
the world with idiotic cornflakes
There are three lies still alive
Freedom, Democracy and Human Rights

Author notes
I want you to merge words that don't make sense and make ideas out of vocabulary that otherwise, means nothing. Nonsense with purpose. Random words that together make a coherent statement. Or maybe the words mean nothing but each reader finds their meaning in the garbled mess.

Dress Rehearsals

All through the seasons
nature sheds the attire.

we change clothes
in everyday life,
retire clothless

Births and deaths
are dress changes.

 Unattached

Life is an attachment to the past
Any action that is the past, present or future
are according to a blueprint,
for an action plan drawn with a flow chart.
All the attributes of the body mind and intellect
is an adaptor goes a long way,
tagged with bondage.

In the entanglement of the labyrinth of time
we stress and strain the sticky strings
attached with the intention of a reward!
Wife, children, family, possessions
live in the mind for a long time,

the wisdom dawns on you when
the futile worldly wealth possessed
turns out to be the just figure of a dream.
The wise ones get out of the dragnet soon,
dispossess the world right away.
Fly away to freedom as doves of love and peace
Freedom from strings of fear is liberation

I Sigh Deeply

I have the moon in my stomach
tickling my body and senses.
Looking at the stars I sigh deeply.
Fond memories drench my eyes.
My soul weeps for your fondle

My Prisoner

He was my brain teaser
Wrecked and stole my grey cells.
Hacked me all through life to hell.
Today I caught him redhanded in jail

Beauty

I have been in the solitude
watching the lake silently.
Observed her many faces.
expressions changed
every moment of the day.
When the sun retired
she had a wave of emotions
her face turned red
lips glowed on a drop of sunlight.

Vermilion on her forehead
spread on her face.
Her eyeshades shone
as she moved her eyelashes.
mascara shaded her eyes
Deep blue eyes showed the depth of her soul
.

Pupils swam like fish
she spread her blue hair In the pool
danced with waves in the lake.
took a dip in the
the serenity of the cool ambience.

Moon too jumped in the lake
flooding the shore with tides of beauty.
A cosmic subtle music rises in the mind

moment to moment
I follow the soft footfall of silence,
as I rest my head on the lap sleep,
caressing she kissed my eyes.
The beauty of silence envelopes my mind

Mind Blogs

here is a little box inside hidden from the vision
A kicking vibing casket once was empty but a tick.

Now It is full and flooding stuffed with galaxies.
It is an ornate little container pumping lifeblood into life.
Thoughts, visions, images, names, and forms are hidden in
the good, bad and ugly lives here in peace.
Sometimes Pandora opens her collection to look at.
To her surprise, the mind blogs and one by one all stuff escapes.

While calming her mind she shuts it suddenly
the calmness prevails, star of hope shines.

Eyes glow with wonder, the mystery reveals
Prometheus lights a fire in the human hearts
Dream of life warms up and turns into a fine flame

The Need of the Time

Here is the world moving fast-rolling, sighing, coughing for breath
The horizon is littered with clouds of yesterday, today and tomorrow
somebody is pouring black ink, It seeps slowly all over the world
Negativity covers the face of the earth, as the sun had retired behind
the smog
Faded stars try to get up from hangovers, dawn still to arrive from a
deep
slumber. The sea is lashing on the shore with the oil slick.

Seagulls and starfish litter the beach denoting human greed
Time stands still on the rocky cliff. Lifting the veil of darkness a beam
of sunlight falling on the beach, there is a sprinkle of rain against
Slowly a rainbow is forming with its exquisite splendour.

My tearful eyes shine suddenly reflecting and refracting soothing
the seventh symphony of colours. seeing the rain clouds depart.
mind blooms with a bow of colours I wish I could arch a rainbow in
every mind infusing the colour of love. The need of the time

From the Solitude of Time

From the solitude of time
She came in a bubble of divinity.
Nature was carrying her in the womb
of celestiality.

Holding the umbilical cord of love
she came on earth silently.
Floating on the wings of beauty.
From the gondola of the holy halo
she dreamed of the future.
Splashed herself in the ocean of grace
Swam to the shore of life.

Placing her aura of ecstasy
on the beach of humanity
she placed her footprints.
Became mother earth
Feeding her children with the nectar of compassion
as the mother of all beings and nonbeings.
Caressing her children on her lap
with a melodious lullaby, she made us
sleep in the comforts of her warmth

The Twinkle in the Eyes

The rain makes a stopover
making clouds of dust rest.
She left making dots,
rolling crystal drops on leaves cascade.

The child smiles, and her gum glows
two milk teeth shine.
Have you ever seen such a cute smile?
A smile of god from the soul of nature.

The breeze dries the raindrops
wet sand sticks on soles.
Freshened with rain, the shrubs
nod softly with recouped energy.

Nature whistles a song
My little puppy wags his tail
He rolls on the sand
See him smile too

The clouds move at a slow pace
looking down
Sun bows down to the sea.
I sketch a portrait of nature
so pure, so innocent
so lively with a twinkle
in the eyes.

Song of Silence

In the silence
In the solitude
In total retreat
Evolves the magnanimity of purity.
There is no high or low tide of emotions.
No waves.
The sea is dead
Across the dead sea
The pyre is lit
Bathing in the brightness of fire
the enlightened souls dance
Then gets into a trance
the knowing the known and knowledge dissolves
into the fold of silence.
The verse of silent soliloquy pervades.
Again the first divine sound
echoes through AUM
The poem of silence!

The Exotic Arena

The sky falls in the river
the colour of the evening sky spreads
The water moves slowly
spreading the hues
The sun had already washed
his dirty linen
hanged on the horizon.
The Breeze
swings the line to dry
Pulling the curtain the moon
Just showed his face.
Stars are dressing up
for the show
the river is streaming slowly
along with the sighs of the tide
I take a deep breath to invoke
the exotic arena.
dive deep into the serenity
merging with the flow.
I don't know if I used
cliche at all
my imagination
caught the ambience

One Day I Will

He made a cage around me
with golden railings,
fed me with emotions
sold his love with a string.
I never thought it was
a string attached.
slowly he grabbed my freedom,
my identity,
my entity.
He carried me around
exhibited,
turning me into a parrot.
I became his slave
eating his desires.
One day
I will
fly away into freedom.
holding his body
in my beak.

Ignore Them

Cruelty has only one face of facelessness
Darkness, of mind, thoughts and action
In this world of duality and multiplicity,
we find some skunks running around stinking the air.

From time immemorial the same happenings
Jesus, Lord Krishna, Gandhiji and much more
They all were persecuted for the fulfilment of dark visions
Yet, they endured and showed a flame torch for us

Let us not hide behind cowardice,
Let us fight, fight for our freedom, for our children
for humanity. let us fight with the sword of courage.
They are nothing but maggots that breeds
in the filthy carcass of their mind and time, Ignore them!

Time Oblivion

On the cliff of my mind,
there stands a lone edifice
I stand on an edge of my thoughts
there she stands my heritage home.
my mental retreat, a resort, and an asylum
for my mental recharge.
Nostalgic memories rise me up
from the graveyard of modernity.

The mansion is a historic monument
of many generations,
who lived there with pomp and prestige.
All great-grandparents lived and ruled here.
We, children, had whale of a time
brothers, sisters, and cousins all played
in their fantasy games,
fought over for a gooseberry.

Each room and wall witnessed
good and bad times
sadness and happiness
each room is echoed with laughter
and weeping.
the pain of births and deaths
the happiness of mothers and their smiles
when the first baby was born.

There were marriages and birthdays,
Deaths and mourning.
There is a lingering smell of life
in the four walls of each room,
the aroma of life.
The smell of sweat and hair oils
The old hardened pillows talk
about the heads rested on it.
That emits the murmur of husband and wife
when they made love.

The echoes of crying babies
The old smell of Coaltar soap
Spit marks outside the wall
having the reddish colour of Beetlejuice.
All these aromatic mixtures of smells
bring the nostalgic memories of faded
life and time oblivion in my mind!

Journey To

I am just a flower bud,
who travelled from
infinity to the unknown
to bloom at a time
that was destined.
The journey continued
until the arrival
of the spring.
In an unaware moment
the flower opened her eyes,
blossomed with freshness
and fragrance.
Time moves ahead
kicking
each moment becomes stale already,
and future uncertain.
I was consumed
by the big mouth.
Each nanosecond
carries the entire galaxy
to a future
the ejected and dropped out
lie flat decaying
basking in the sun
waiting for a reverse
transmutation!
Entropy

Invisible Walls

All we live in a maze
surrounded by high walls.

As soon as the baby is born
We make a fuss
start building
many physical
and invisible walls around.
place the child
in a cradle covered with a net
warm clothes another one
restricted to visitors
is a wall against infection.

Parents, society, nation
countries, laws
all add walls against
freedom of life
and movements.

Religious walls
caste, creed walls
the colour of the skin walls
taboos, rites
all are grand walls
bigger and longer than
great wall of China

we erect special fencing
around men and women

Ultimately we turn ourselves,
a Hippie and walks in a huff
fly away into freedom,
demolishing all the high rise
built up of time

Mask of My Sorrow

Bit by bit
the dark tongue
consumes me
I lose myself
daily in a scuffle
with a mad comet.

The werewolves
snap my flesh.
some of it
floats and flows
through the milky Way.

My laughing face
is a mask of sorrow
my tears stream
as a rivulet
into the world

I weep shamelessly
but no one hears
It is a curse
that I have to
live with

Comparing me with
an idol of love
is misnomer
Just watch for
my howl
in the silence of
night
It is an expression
of my fear
of losing another piece
of my flesh
I lose it daily
until I dissolve
in the whirlpool
of darkness

Again to be reborn
on a full moon day!

Will Discard Him One Day

I have a big
labyrinth of the mind.
He prompts
my dialogues
in the world.
Often intervenes,
misguides,
my noble and wise
decisions.
Makes me utter
untruth.
Will discard
him one day!

You Are Liberated

We trekked through
the time many times.
A baby is born
with an empty mind.
Becomes a rag picker
having a garbage sack,
a mind junkyard
dumped with desires, collected
from waste bins of the past.
We go on filling
Time to depart suddenly
to fill the cause and effect
To fulfil the dreams of past
another birth!
The cycle goes on...
to a dry-fried seed
no sprouts are possible now.
You are liberated
from rebirth.

The Demigods

Centenarians arrived
with a piece of heaven
in their wings.
They got their flying colours
and wings as
space shuttle pilots
when they completed
a century of age in their life.

Came to planet earth
as tourists to celebrate
the great achievement.

When the entire world
was sleeping
the aliens partied
all night
on the wings of
intoxication,
fanned and fluttered
wings of joy till dawn.

The rejoicing frenzy
lasted until dawn
ending up in their marriage!
to become Humans
instead of their higher rank
back home" the Demigods"

it was a bungee jump
from the cliff unknown
tied on a string
of illusion
swinging
to grab
you
back

We Had Built an Emotional Bridge

We had built an emotional bridge
through the time together.
Had a dream painted in my mind
You visited my fairyland often.
As a glaze of sunlight lit my face
I saw you in the depth of my eyes
as the wave of my hopes.
You lit my moon and stars with a smile.

Then one day we fought for silly nothing.
You left me in a huff and never turned back.
Don't you know it was a love bug fight?

Oh, I Don't Know

The soul is the diamond
hidden inside on a pedestal
of eternal platonic love,
unstrung.

A sweet silent smile
always flower infinitely
on the face
Once near the master
you do not want anything
just a hug and kiss at his feet.

Your sorrow flows
off your eyes unaware
all you fillip in the mind
gets dried
you leave your master
with an empty mind
pain subsided
You forget past and future
live in him now.
and a shining face,
that glow is a smile
of your soul!

After some time
one learns to accept
all dualities of life.
Good, bad, ugly, hot and cold,
pain and happiness.
The thoughts are balanced
the laughter of tranquil
on the face of whatever.

Now one can
understand the futility
of the fighting mind.
Love percolates
from your bosom
To one and all
without any bias.
You shine in every heart
that you meet, man or animal
You are the one soul
that shines in everyone
they also live in you
as a part of the whole universe

OH, I don't know
what have I written?

Star of a Dream 1

Prologue
A Star of a Dream
just fell on earth
from the hands of god.

Oh my God,
where am I?
who pushed me down
to this unknown place?
Oh where is my
a cord of love?
food channel
what is the place
I don't like the smell
I can't bear this
powerful light over my head.

Oh where is my mom
I was safe and secure
in her stomach
Oh my, what am I doing?
I am breathing
fresh what is it?
Why so many
masked creatures
around me?

Oh, my god, they cut
my food tube too
No No, don't.
Do not hold me
upside down.
I promised
I will not cry.
But I have to.
Open my sound box
ngre ngre ngre............
Is it my sound?

Yes now they are doing
something for me.
I am near my Mom
Ohh mommy oh mommy
am I safe?
I see a flower bloom
on the lips of my mother!
how does she do that?
Oh yes, I learned.
My first smile
to the world
from the Lord!

Epilogue
Now I am cuddled
in the warmth of love
Oh, dear Mommy!
I feel safe!

The Only One

She came in search of her entity
trekked and strolled all through planets,
Imagined and scanned the entire universe,
talked with stars, the moon, and the sun
danced with asteroids a long way.

I Swam in a milky way and chatted with swans.
At the end of a dream, she tumbled
cascaded to the earth
she stuck in a cobweb of time
got rooted as a seed of the future.

Among the wilderness of forest
she grew into a ravishing wild beauty.
As if in meditation she invoked
the mood and character of nature.

Enchantments followed her soul
she reverberated in the solitude.
When she smiled the region smiled
ambience got intoxicated.
The entire forest chanted with her.
She became one with nature.
At last, she found her identity
She is the mother the one only one!

Yes I Am a Cusp

I dream like a Scorpion
Just hiding behind my simple life
Try to live in the silence of my solitude.
Love to stretch my muscles if I have to,
With a sting of my words, to make sure
both are not hurt, yet I hit strong.
I want nothing extraordinary
but I love to live in the cosiness of my laziness.

Not to be disturbed by mundane life
I care and create a love for others.
But I select very few friends
I keep them with me always
irrespective of the duration we meet.
I remember every bit of their help
never forget them even if they forget.
I never wish for anything that is not mine
I can not cheat or steal anybody
I feel dirty when I possess anything, not mine.
Not caring for any fancy of the day.
I just love to be left alone in the crowd
loneliness is my company too
there I interact with myself,
and can decide what is best for me.
Do you think I am a CUSP?
yes I am born op 19 /Nov
I am an introverted and misunderstood person

The Garden of Love

Once before the Britishers colonized this heart of the earth.

We spoke about" Lokaha Samastha Sukhino Bhavanthu"

Let every being and nonbeing live in peace and harmony.

Fight for blood and eye for an eye, tooth for a tooth was unknown.

Our forefathers taught us to fight for justice in peace

Fight for righteousness without fear and timidity.

Freedom is fearlessness in completing the duty.

The great Mahatma Gandhi did that and taught the world

Non-violence and fasting until death to achieve

the heart of self and win the heart of others too.

He successfully practised the philosophy of Lord Krishna to attain freedom.

Once a fashionable man transformed to the attire of poor, loin cloth

Freed himself from materialism to spirituality

Made the British empire falls at his feet of love.

He never fought the British, yet he fought the cruelty.

He was not at war with anybody, but he was at war with himself

As Jesus said he showed his right face to slap and the left too

He preached and practised Karma Yoga as Lord Krishna's utterance

Of Bhagavath Geetha, He did his job without any craving for results.

His life became a living example of Geetha's philosophy

Often proclaimed the famous declaration of Jesus

My father's house has many mansions

He went on proving his life" The story of my experiments with truth"

He left the world with an everlasting chant "Hey Ram"

with an arrow shot at the heart of the world's conscience.

This is the philosophy of India
We have nothing to give to the world except our love for all
Love, Peace, Harmony
Let a thousand flowers bloom in the heart, the garden of love!

The Divine Molecule

An atom explodes
The divine molecular wave
travels on to eternity.
Unending journey beyond time and space,
an expanding space into infinity.
I created a web of compassion
where all live as a particle of my dream
enact a role in the dream of destiny.
A fate undescribed but live
as a part of natural laws.
The Maya, my potent part
manifests in and out
as macro and microcosm
One day I shut your eyes
ending the magic of life.
Let you dive into the secret of death.
On that day all have to return home,
from the unforeseeable distance, where ever.
It is a trek back home.

One fine day I withdraw
the dream.
the spider vacuums the net.
He retires into yogic sleep.
and floats in the deluge of time.
The entire galaxies live

through the breath of time
passes through my nostrils several aeons
I declare there is nothing
in this world except for my dream.
The seer, scene, and scenery are mine
The one truth, that is the ultimate
THE DIVINE MOLECULE

The Painter

The sun
threw away
his
palette
and crayons
into the horizon
before taking
a dive in the ocean.

Breeze
brushed n'
sketched
a painting
of his heart's
content

The Truth

The world is living
in little islands
submerged in the
Ocean of time.

The deluge
slowly consumes
everything
wise men stay afloat
keeping the tranquil
retire in the
meditative sleep
on the shore of
bliss.

Some grow into infinity
beyond time
and space.
They are the ones who
has seen the past
present and future
Have transcended
everything
to become the ideal
of an idol.
They retain the meaning

of meanings
The truth.
we look at them
with awe
bow our heads in worship
their gracefulness.

Was It a Dream?

Depth of night
further sank me into
a deep slumber.
Rumbling rain
and seeping coolness
pushed me further
into a deep sleep.

Suddenly I found myself
in a space suit
sitting in front of a
cockpit with innumerable
dials and gauges.
A commander on duty.
There are other three
astronauts too.

we are on a mission
to space.
I was watching the screen
communication with the
tracking centre.

Through the windows
I was watching outside
the shuttle is

flying fast in
Hypersonic speed
we were pumping
the fuel in a beautiful tail
behind us.

The scenery outside
are thrilling and awesome
There were stars moon and
asteroids at our touching
distance.
we pushed the puffy clouds
down.
Far away I can see the
Earth glowing in
emerald green.
The golden glow of the moon
and planets,
a comet just passed over our
space shuttle.

After some time
we went on a spacewalk
touched the space
with our bare hands
swam in the mystery.

we had crossed millions
of miles at the speed of light.

Suddenly
I saw Kalpana Chawla
making a swim.
I saluted her.
Then I heard Sunita Williams
chatting online

Sudden I was pushed
away from my spacecraft
I was floating
in the space.
My spacecraft had gone
when I opened my eyes
I was recovering from
a fall from the cot
Was it a dream?

 The chill of November
slowly creeping into blankets.
cuddle closer into the warmth
hugging the warmth of her body
Dawn is still far away hiding behind the fog
Sun is getting ready combing his golden hair.
Soon the warm glints of sunlight fall on earth
The morning theatre is gettings ready for the show
Soon the singing birds will arrive with a celestial voice
I just love to listen to songs tossing under this blanket
The hangover of last night still litters the room
Dreams of beautiful lovemaking embrace the thoughts
The lights of yesterday's winter party still wink at the morning mist
The day has, to begin with, a happy note, the start of a lazy weekend!

The Mirror That Reflects the World

The labyrinth of time and life
binds to choke the mind.
breath almost stops in the windpipe
the mundane life irritates
the thoughts climb the wilderness.
desires and emotions flood.
a deluge lashes on the shore of the mind.
somewhere in the remoteness
A lone sound rises above the senses

Somebody inside shouts
break away from the chains, and be free.
While sitting on a mat of uncertainty
the mind shouts with all negativity.

A sound from inside makes you hear
It says to listen and guides you to the murmur
of your soul. the enchantments follow
You fall into the depth of unknown peace of compassion
The world disappears behind the memories,
retreats into an attempted silence.
You visualize all the good things
The mind flows in tears of happiness
Now you are resting your thoughts
in the fold of your divinity.
All the thoughts merge into oneness

All images disappear into truth
Time stands still at your beck and call
The bliss of love dawns on you
You become one with the ultimate
the truth is nothing but the truth
You become the epicentre of love.
The mirror that reflects the world

Mystery of Universe

He is burning himself

to burst

and become

a flame

soon his halo

will die

he will be

a black star

compressed

into a black hole

once a brilliant

star on the horizon

slowly fades

from order

to disorder

The mystery

of universe

entropy

To the Day of Life

Metal bubbling in the forge
smoke and fume speeds
clouding as fog.
The golden glow emits off the hearth
creates a halo on the horizon.
Dawn just gets off the sea
still, the sleep hangs in the eyes.

The ambience changes every second
the master painter
sketches the face of the universe.
Silos filled with golden grains
sighs with happiness.

All forms of paintings on display
real, surreal, cubic, murals of nature.
Mind blogs at the wonder of a cosmic dream
Somewhere a tune from the flute
The breeze caresses my thoughts
mesmerized by the magic
I stand awestruck.
Beauty percolates through
the veins imagination.
Whistling a tune of the soul
I retreat to the day of life.

A Selfie

He is writing a poem
on the horizon
taking a snapshot
in black and white clouds
litter around his halo
takes a selfie with
stars and billows of time.

A fog just arrives
in front of the vision
Today is a special day
he comes closer to earth
to give a warm kiss
on the face of night
horripilate globe
with a wild kiss after
the long seventy years
of loneliness
The night blooming
jasmines will open their souls
spreading the aroma
of lovely feelings.

The emotions will
flow flooding
as a tide of divinity.

Mind rests
with a noble thought
of creativity sketched
in black and white
on an imaginative canvas!

Damocles

The world is on the move
since then
revolutions, renaissance
Reformation.
the wheels of civilization
rolled many centuries.
life made easy,
then grabbed by greed.
we forgot to kiss the baby.
mother and father
tied to machines.
values are flat.
wheels rusted
the pushcart is struck
Damocles
sleeping in the param
unaware of the danger.

Tower of Babel

The Stairway to Heaven
built with pride and prestige
Man made it into a huge column
the structure of might
The Tower of Babel
the magnanimity of mankind.
the citadel was unique
raised beyond imagination
decor with stars and comets
spoke the language of humans
a space station to study
the expanse of the universe

a lightning strikes
the edifice fizzles out
disintegrated into thousands of pieces
now we are speaking
the language of Discord
The united nations of the
world of greed and hate!

She Is the Mother of All

She is the mother of all mothers
A manifestation of nature
Every being and non-beings
lives in the womb of time
embraces the world with love
invokes beauty from heaven
creates the excellence of perfection
exhales her grace in every creature
she is the mother of all
in every hue of compassion
She is the mother of all.

Lord Star

When highlighted by coloured spotlights,
Most of the dark shades hide behind.
A star of brilliance guides you through.
The troubled turbulence of a rough sea.

Light of Knowledge

Unknown unaware of this world
thrives in the effulgence of light of lights
every soul is lime lighted from the source of compassion
there is no place that it does not reach.

Every nook and corner gets the brilliance of delight
a spec of a spark just makes life visible
when the light fades the eyes get drowned
the dark wings of nightfall on life

The journey of life is to reach the reality
the reach- back into the enlightenment,
eliminating the silhouetted darkness.
The lotus meditates all night for the sun
at dawn, he arrives to bless the world to bliss.

The dew rests on the petal of the lotus
gets dried into the ecstasy of nothingness.
Time gets dried before the globule
awareness of incandescence lustre
makes you dance with the truth.

The realization of the truth of emptiness
stretches your hands to embrace the world
into the fold of the permanent luminescence
to become one with eternal peace unaware,

delving on the pedestal of lotus stigma.
The light of knowledge emits unstrung love for all.

Camphor lit in my heart burns full without
any sediments. Wonder if life was like that!

Tunes of Life

My soul is singing
a celestial tune
harping on the
sinews of my thoughts

I hear the cosmic
music echoing
from the strings
of divine love

I hear the flute
from the depth
of my mind
there the lord
plays the flute
streaming his
compassionate notes

I tune the
imagination
to the images
of the played
to awake you
from the depth
of darkness

I feel his lips
flowing
into the delight
of musical flow
of life
and the bliss
of divine
singing.

My Dream

The celestial melody flows
From the memory of infinity
My mind harps on the strings
Of the Soul of the divine symphony

Merged in the subtle solitude
I invoke the muse into my soul
Invisibly she forges my senses
Flows incessantly off to the world

Horripilation tap dance in cosmic tunes
She becomes the flow of ambrosia
Her mind streams as a rivulet
Drenching and quenching the dryness

Behind every unblemished blue shade
The music and rhythm meditate
The soul manifests as a spontaneous lyric
Streaming as a subtle rhythm live.

Let me embrace my purity
Merge and stay deeply rooted in the earth
Rooted deep to explore raw earth
Drink from water springs, burn
Exhaust in the magnanimity of azure sky.

Listen to It

Unaware of a touch of God
through the brush of an artist.
a fine stroke of the brush bristle
a compassionate glow,
on every object of the subject.
A shade of a theme colour
The painter inside creates
a world of bloom exquisite,
gives his life breathed into it.
The painting talks in silence.
Listen to it.
You will hear the music
the lovely music of heaven

Husky Blissful Moan

Wilderness of nature
Walking towards
raw manliness
to get fondled
caressed
and embraced
into the fold
of macho.

Man and woman
explores,
tastes the
exotic forbidden
honey-dripping fruit.

Nature whistles
a song
from the soul.
A divine
symphony of
beauty and love
enchanted in the sweet
Husky blissful moan
of the night-wind

Vantablack Mind

You are sinking
In a whirlpool of
dark storm
Gasping
heaving for air
eyes blacked out
Breath stops
a tsunami hits
your memories
collapse into depth,
Into vantablack mind.
Own creation of
darkness (99.96)
blackest

A Dark Shade of History

A shadow fight
goes on
mudslinging
acrimony
bleeding
tail biting
cruelty on
women and children
men die
of torture
their tombs
war memorials
veterans
At last
the shadow
maker
loses his grip
he becomes
a dark shade
of History
a shot in the buttocks

Reflections

With a thousand anklets
feet chiming on the shore
nature is floating on her back
shaking the feet sprinkling
silvery droplets all around.
Smiling, she dives in the
the serenity of the azure water.
The sky looks into
the mirror of the ocean.

The virgin beach is waiting
for the first step caress her.
With bareback she lies
basking lazily in the sun
body shining with Sun-cream.

Soon the beach will be crowded
men and women in their colourful
swim trunks and bikinis,
sipping fruit cocktails.

Every moment the scenery
changes on the horizon.
I watch the reflection on her face.
A romantic hum of an old tune
makes me cuddle in the
the warmth of her smile.

An Embrace of Peace

Nature dives here
into the depth of purity
silently she floats
in meditation
moving slowly on
a backstroke.
serenity lives here
On the shore of
solitude.
every drop of water
splashes a pearl
into the depth of
my mind.

every grain of sand
glitter on the bed
golden granules.

the sky looks
her makeup,
spills blue of her beauty
on the lake.
her blue eyes dance
on the surface
making ripples
with round waves.
like a kiss

I empty my mind
to see my reflection.
it has become
crystal clear like clean
water
I take a dip in the depth of purity
feeling the soul of the lake
an embrace of peace.

Just Enough Time to Live

There is no time for anything.
It is a busy life
Weekends for
makeover.
Free time for
personal hygiene
laundry.
I eat breakfast
in the car.
what you need
two slices
and a cup of black coffee.
Lunch at the office
grabs a sandwich.
long drive back
a couple of drinks
burger and coke
for supper.
what more does one need
in life!
Just enough time
to live!

The Aroma of Christ

Another drizzle
A splash of snowflakes
A little lump of ice
Tumble off the pine
A squirrel peeps out of the hideout
Her mink shines with golden beads
Divine aroma spreads
Goosebumps send heat waves.

Blissful steps of nature
Far from the mountains
A divine star smile
Filling the Valley of Dreams
With celestial grace.
A shepherd moves in tidy steps
Holding a calf under his warmth

Somewhere rises a laughter
A choir from the church
A sledge ground to halt
A red glow on the ice floor
I kneel placing a cross of thoughts
The aroma of fresh baked
I withdraw my pen to ink
My merry Christmas dreams.

My Pen Falls Silent

Once, my pen was filled
full with sensitive, sentimental words
I had it adorned with twinkles
studded with glowing grains

I was searching for something,
an effulgent aromatic creation
from the Soul of Aesthetics
Just for fun creating a mural of the creator

The curator of my idol of art was in deep slumber
I sent my vocabulary horses to hoof around
they ran like stallions in a wild race
I tamed my words with a whip of discretion

I talked about, emotions, love, sensitivity,
sentiments, and meditative vocabulary
At last, I invoked her spirit with a passion
She rose elegantly in her best attire

My muse took a dip in the pool of my words
played a long time with my soulful images
They embraced their ecstatic souls
reincarnated in my words as a muse of imagery dreams

My pen fell silent
My idols smashed
I became free
floating in the sky as a kite.
while my muse holds
the string of imagination.

Oasis

Over the ocean,
a mirage glides past.
On the desert of the mind, too.
Sand waves run haste
Trekking dunes
through windy deserts.
A strong hurricane develops,
desert storm.
Fearful gusty dust wind
sea heaves high mountainous.
The sky comes down
entire star and the moon
takes a dive
the planets float, like a shipwreck
My thoughts dived
into the cobalt-green sea.

A camel slowly leaps and creep
the sand mountains
my imagination swings
on his back.
I see an oasis in my vision
filled with fresh springs.

Then I dived deep into the ocean floor
my words swam over coral gardens
flora and fauna
of seabed.
Flowering corals and cuttlefishes
I scribble a poem on a red coral cliff

Breathe fresh air
under the shade of a date palm grove.

Art of Nature

Let it snow
An art deployment
On the face of the earth
The natural artist
showers grey blue
sub-zero granules
from the grace of the season

The painter uses only one
unique colour from his
soul,
the grey-blue ice flakes
silvery blue grains.
With his brush
whatever he touches
turns into frost
becomes an aesthetic
lively sculpture

the entire ambience
transforms
to a heavenly artwork

each object
gets covered in crystal
and gleam in the gloom

snow carpeted the earth
hides behind
the magic wand of winter

The sculpturer
whistles a tune,
the valley nods
with tapping feet

when the first
light of summer
arrives
the entire art display
merges with the
painter,
becoming a rainbow
in a palette.

A Colourful
fragrant
spring springs
from heaven
with
shower of
confetti's
all around
the valley

The Grandeur

Mighty ocean
rolls, waves, heaves high
dances with a breeze
dive deep and
wash her hair
Her anklets lie onshore
tingling in the wind
sometimes roar,
lie down low at tides

She houses a lot of
lively living sensations
a vast colony of
wonders housed
under her mystery
of heart.
On the floor lie
scattered the wrecks of
mighty past, history,
marines, battleships
treasures,
and above all
an unknown wonder
the shiny pearl of her soul.

The sun retreats
in her bosom

When she sighs
moon peeps
off her beauty.
litter of moonlit
surround

The storm of nature
raise her above
carrying on mountainous wings.
she remains a mystic mystery
yet to be explored
there is a lively
kicking, tweaking, world
inside her.

She opens her heart
of wonders
like a divine
revelation,
the grandeur
of compassion
when invoked.

On a sensual
astral Moon trip
Found a
Soft spot.
Still exploring
The mystery

Tail of Scorpio

A man never
bothered about greying
Loves dew covered the world
have a tail of Scorpio
stings badly if attacked
Just leave me alone
in the serene solitude
of laziness.

Rhythmic Drumming

Perfection
lives
behind light
and shades.

Aesthetic
mind
pastures
on contour's
rhythmic
drumming
 fall in the sea
floats
The old man
caught them in net
happy catch
he towed his boat
to shore

No Regrets

When you learn
subtracting
Zeroing
Life is easy
No regrets

I Made a Magic Box

I made a magic box
Out of a hardboard,
fridge pack
made it into a hideout
a secret space
for unfolding my dreams

Over the top
made holes
of different diameters

Over my head
Watched azure
night sky
glitters with stars,
the moon, and planets
Suddenly the entire sky
falls into the sea
floats
I saw
Uncle moon
Swimming in the sea
catching them in the net
One by one

happy catch!
towed his boat
to shore

I closed
my dream house
housing
the catch

One With Time

Solitude lives here
In the sanctity of silence

Nature embraces time
Showering ambrosia of love
Wisdom manifests with
a celestial brilliance

Serenity sweeps the murmur
Of mind
Fluttering dry leaves of thoughts
Combed to muted soliloquy
The best of the moment
Drizzles cool pulchritude
Awesome nature rocks in a chair
Of wisdom

Mountainous wisdom erects
A canopy of comfortable shade
Let my thoughts meditate
To merge the elegance of
The calm and peaceful lake of tranquillity.

Come rest here on the lap of infinity
Merge to delve
In the sea of unity
Become one
With the frozen time.

Colour of Purity

Every sound
each colour and hue
emerges from one notation
One sound, one syllable
ultimately
all the blaze and blare
merges into one monotone
The song of silence

Rainbow shades
fizzle out
sieve through the rain
and litter exotic pigments
everywhere on earth

lately
becomes one flow
One hue
the purest immaculate
all colours merge
into one reality
the pigments of truth

the idea of life
is to reach
the colourless colour

crystalline purity
the transparent white
where the soul
emerges to be one
with reality
the field of identity
without entity

First Step

Step ladder
to the mystery
of life and death
begins
the first step
taken
Out there
the infinity
awaits
with stretched hands
Music of silence
welcomes you
to the land
of immortality
come! soon

To Explode Into Ecstasy

Smooth flow of music
streams from heaven
the rhythm, rhyme,
beats and tunes cascade
as silky emotions glide

Ambrosia from
the realms of mystery.
love merges with
passion streaks.

Bodies glide down
to the point of bliss
contours measured
and aroused.

The murmur of tongues
lips shiver
each cell wants to
explore and explode
bodies quiver

They do not want
to separate
holding on to remain
in the fire
to explode into
ecstasy

 Goodbye

From the moment of birth, life is pushed on a train of time.
Stuffed in a compartment life is enacting a drama.
You interact to complete your dialogue in a role
Leaving everything, every bondage alights at your destination.

He Survived Tornado

Silently he watched a thief
entering his premises
As a doctor, he was helpless
and desperately viewing
the situation, a nightmare

Life changed through
many twists and turns.
Looked at the blank eyes
of his wife, confronting her
with a remotely distanced look

He watched thousands of
crabs fighting and eating
every cell of his bones
loosened feeble muscles
bitten by steroids, chemo.
and radiated dry emotions

Our prayers are answered
he survived the tornado

A Tasteless Song

Like a tornado,
it appears from nowhere
with a black flag of a skull, n' bones hoisted,
waving against any wind of time.

A strong calm moonlight
touches the deck
exposing the pirate's booty,
high waves leap up
sounding disgusted.

Black criminal eye patches
create a semi-dusk even dawn.
Sighting the horror
seagulls depart with a flutter
with a tasteless song.